PASS THE WORD

A Mindset Transformation to Fulfillment and Spirituality

DeNita L. Turner
&
John K. Jenkins, Sr.

Foreword by Joseph F. Lewis

PASS THE WORD

A Mindset Transformation to
Fulfillment and Spirituality

DeNita L. Turner
&
John K. Jenkins, Sr.

Published in the United States of America All rights reserved

Pass the Word: A Mindset Transformation to Fulfillment and Spirituality

© 2019 by DeNita L. Turner and John K. Jenkins, Sr. Requests for information should be addressed to:

passtheword@denitaturner.com

ISBN: 978-0-578-21387-3

Library of Congress Control Number: 2018966970

Published by DL Turner Consulting, Richmond, VA

Edited by The Comprehensive Editing, Writing & Publishing Company, LLC and KWE Publishing LLC

Dedication

To my parents, Joseph and Joan Lewis. Thank you for your "unwavering" love. So proud to be your daughter!

DeNita

&

To my parents, John and Lucy Jenkins. So thankful I'm your son,

John

Contents

FOREWORD

by Joseph F. Lewis, proud father

My foreword is a story about a shy little girl who grew up in the small town of Appomattox, Virginia—my daughter and one of the authors of this book, DeNita L. Turner. This same girl (I call her "girl" because that's what she will always be to me) has gone from being a shy girl to a business woman who engages professional athletes, college students, corporate executives and transitioning individuals. She helps them build confidence and solidify a positive image.

It's amazing how things can change. Over the years, I watched her grow personally, professionally and spiritually. During all of that, one of my wife's and my happiest days is the day she called and said, "I found my church. It's a little church on a side street, known only by a few people, with barely enough room to park your car. The name of it is First Baptist Church of Glenarden."

The long-lasting history of her attending that church, from its small beginnings to its mega church status with over 11,000 members, resulted in many things, including discovering that she and her pastor, John K. Jenkins, Sr., worked with people with many similarities. Additionally, DeNita and her pastor crossed paths in sports with the goal of uplifting and inspiring others through words and deeds. Several years of discussing their desire to encourage people eventually led to their wanting to share their belief in the power of influence that words have, whether that influence is good or bad.

I have also had the privilege to observe Pastor Jenkins embrace a new idea for a book, become a motivator to share what he knows about the power of words, as well as become a mentor to my daughter, not to mention once again help find an

1

additional way to spread the Word.

My wife Joan and I are proud and humble to see their work over the years culminate in the publication of *Pass the Word*. This book has made us smile, cry and reflect on how we both use words. We hope it does the same for you.

PREFACE

H ave you heard any of the following statements? Better yet, have you ever spoken any of them yourself?

"Over my *dead* body!" "He makes me *sick*."

"If they see me in this awful hair style, I'll just *die*."

"My kid will always be *lazy*. He'll never amount to much,

just like his father." "*I can't* do it."

"This won't work, *no matter what I do*."

"I'm *going to get the flu* this year. I just know it." "Everything's *falling apart* on me."

In our respective capacities as life coach to corporate employees, collegiate and professional athletes, and as a pastor of a church in a major metropolis, we hear people speak words like these all the time. In fact, one of the things we both notice in our work is that people have little idea of the power of their words. It doesn't matter that many of our constituents have been exposed to multiple lessons on how the power of their words impacts their lives, they still fail to use word choices to better their lives. Our collective opinion is this: when you're not blessing your life with your words, you're limiting yourself. Which brings us to why we wrote this book.

There are a couple of reasons that motivated us to collaborate on the power of word choice. First, we felt people need an alternative to negative speak. This book is a tool to show them how to cut out negative word choices and replace them with ones that seed life.

Additionally, writing this book was our way to support individuals with information that could assist them with developing a fulfilled life. As we talk to them about their present

3

path versus the one they want to be on, they tend to respond in language that strongly suggests their circumstances will get the best of them, and that they have no power to create a turn-around for themselves. We know that's not true. Yet based on what some of our constituents say, they fail to recognize the power they have over their lives by what they speak. This perspective can change, and it begins with the incredible strength that you have in your tongue. Words matter. Choose yours wisely.

INTRODUCTION

How powerful are your words? Did it ever occur to you that what you speak packs so much power that your words can: either heal or impede wellness, bring positive energy or negative energy to a situation, encourage others or bully them to tears, and even separate lives or rebuild relationships? And, did you know that you even have the power to command your own day by your words alone? That's right. You alone can determine just how well your day will proceed based on whatever you speak. When you consider the awesome power of your tongue, you may begin to seriously realize that you should do what one writer called "taming" the tongue. In our book, we call it contemplating your word choice, and more specifically, deliberately passing those words that create, build, encourage and otherwise inspire.

Let's face it, words have the impact of a bullet or seed (Chapman, 2008). One mindless slip of the tongue and your words can become a reckless force of destruction, denying you the chance to be the positive, influential change agent you were created to be. However, a disciplined, strategic word choice seeds a life of healing energy, support, restoration, motivation, unity, and so on. It sets a course for bridging gaps and closing chasms in relationships not only among people, but also between nations. No wonder it's just good common sense to have executive leadership that is wisely cognizant of the words they speak; otherwise, a single person can inadvertently lead a country into all kinds of chaotic situations that become difficult to resolve and restore order.

Regardless of any of our backgrounds or social standing, the power of our words is not to be underestimated. For certain, what we say matters a *lot*! In just a few pages, you will be introduced to words that can possibly change your present and secure your future—if you use them as we suggest.

A Word about the Word

When we refer to words, we mean specific ones as they impact everyday living. When we consider words from both the Old and New Testaments, we find that they are the revelation of God and His complete expressed will for humanity. Scripture is inspired in thought and its words are infallible, carefully chosen to transcend time and all authority. In a sense, they become the foundation of all truth.

In short, the infallible, authoritative, timeless Word of God builds faith. Unless we contemplate on and speak *His* words, contentment and fulfilled living will always be an illusion. This is why we touch on Scriptures from time to time in this book. We feel it is important that you are grounded in the words God Himself speaks about humanity. He passes on words to us via Scriptures that are full of love and clarity for our lives. Think of it this way: when you speak what God speaks, you come into agreement with His Word, which covers every circumstance, every person, everywhere, every time.

How to Use This Book

We only focus on 12 words in this book, dedicating a chapter to each word. We deliberately did this so that you would have more than enough time to meditate on one word per month through the year. Plus, the words we selected have the propensity to impact you spiritually and in other ways. They are words that we believe will inspire and foster a hunger for a renewed mindset which can only be triggered by reflection and meditation, which brings us to the next point.

Ideally at the start of a new month, you should focus on a new word. During that month, read what we have written on that word. Then, mediate on that word by performing a search on its derivatives and synonyms. You may even want to discover the antonyms of each word so that you are careful in your practice to stay away from using negative word choices to answer life's challenges. Be contemplative of using the word as you reflect on your circumstances, relationships and just everyday living. That is, think about how that word can answer some problem you think has the best of you right now.

Each chapter concludes with a story where the word is presented in practical situations that we feel you may encounter or have already encountered. In these life-like stories, you will see how the characters respond to circumstances by what they speak. Following each story is a set of questions that provoke further thought about the power of your words. As you answer each question, take comfort in the fact that there are no wrong answers, that no one is judging you on anything you write, so be as truthful and transparent as possible. For the *Take Action* section, try to complete each action step in 21 days, as that is the length of time it generally takes to make positive changes.

Finally, we hope this book will motivate you to move to higher heights in your purpose, where you will experience more joy, and, in turn, inspire others as you pass on *the gift of words* and empower them to speak the change they want to see happen.

PREPARATION

There are no secrets to success. It is the result of preparation....

Colin Powell

Prep·A·R a·Tion

*the development of groundwork for a particular
action or process for use or consideration*

1

Our lives follow the pattern of: want it, see it, buy it, consume it. We want our food fast, coffee fast, information fast. Given the rising number of internet sites that offer the opportunity to "find my person," we even want love to come fast. In a few decades, we have gotten to the point where we give less and less consideration to the value of preparing for anything. Life does not happen in a microwave or vacuum. We must learn to embrace preparation to make things happen, which is where a microwave mindset falls short.

Instinctively, some people avoid preparation because they assume it's just way too time-consuming to develop a plan of action to resolve a problem, regardless of its depth. But where would many of our families and successful companies be had they not been guided by business plans or by set goals that took time to be developed and implemented? Just think— preparation led business owners right into wealth, and families into a higher level of security!

Granted, <u>preparation involves a level of rigor</u>. After all, you must take the proper steps to your destiny which may involve a good deal of preparation. There's no way around it, and without it, you will not reach your intended purpose. *Ever.* Nevertheless, some despise the rigorous steps of preparation because they necessitate organized thinking. That is, we have to <u>identify all key issues</u> that we not only should anticipate, but also inevitably deal with if we want to be successful.

If there is anything we have learned in our respective roles as pastor and consultant, it is that critical thinking frequently scares people. This is too bad, because without a critical analysis of how to move from your present circumstances to something better, adequate preparation is almost unavoidable. Yet some are afraid to evaluate their reality tunnel because they want to repress their faults into an unconscious land of no recovery.

Preparation does not happen without planning. It is intentional and strategic with a target, a mission, and an objective—all of which feature you as the focal point. Because it is so critical to success, preparation involves your taking an honest inventory of your strengths and weaknesses. Pause a moment and take a quick inventory right now. What are you good at doing? What are your weaknesses? What do you need to consider in order to reach your ultimate potential?

Once you are aware of your limits, you should not be afraid to acknowledge them as you put together a preparation plan to go after opportunities for change, advancement or success. You see, preparation minimizes the likelihood of fear or terror creeping in and overwhelming your ability to think straight and take charge of your life.

Principles of Preparation

It is just inevitable that some things can never be realized unless we go through the process of preparation. Perhaps a takeaway from this chapter could be: preparation cannot be forged; either you are prepared, or you are not prepared. There are no in-betweens.

Here's something else to think about. The only way you can give your dreams life is to put them through a step-by-step plan where they move from your imagination to actuality. That process is called preparation. Without it, you simply have an active imagination. Your purpose, your reason for being, will remain locked up for good if it is not processed via a plan (i.e., preparation). In essence, preparation gives the inspiration necessary to aim for things that we never thought were possible. However, we know with man things seem impossible, but "with God all things are possible" (Matthew 19:26).

Preparation is a great equalizer. One who is prepared will almost always succeed more than the one who depends on talent alone. Take a guess, if you will, about who is more likely to succeed at taking home, say, an Olympic medal for running a marathon. Will it be the one who prepared with rigorous training, or the one who managed to make the cut by mere skill?

Preparation is so important. Our dreams have no chance of living without it.

A Story about Preparation

Nervously clasping and unclasping his hands, Ray paced up and down the concourse where his plane was still waiting its turn to take to the air. Even though he had flown internationally four different times now, something about leaving the country always made him nervous. The fact that he was finally going to the mountain only made it worse.

He had promised his sister that he would make her dreams come true. Cancer had cut short her life before she ever got to realize her goal of scaling Mount Everest. Ray had spent the past 10 years learning how to climb the world's highest mountain. He had gone from hating climbing up a ladder, to learning how to mountaineer, to scaling the tallest peaks in North America, Europe, and Africa. He loved the focus and strategy required to make a climb. He reveled in the preparations needed for each expedition.

A strong voice pierced the air and announced that his plane was boarding. He took a deep breath as he anxiously waited his turn to get on the plane.

Three days later, Ray was pacing in front of his hotel in Kathmandu. He wanted to scout out the process of loading up for base camp. He was in the first phase of his altitude acclimation plan, taking it slowly. He would head to base camp with his group of climbers in two days. There, he would spend three days at base camp getting his body ready to take on something that spanned the Himalayas. Then, he would finally fulfill his mission to honor his sister.

A smiling, clean-cut man waved at Ray. The gold watch was the first thing that caught Ray's attention.

"Are you headed to Everest base camp?" the man asked.

"Not today. I'm leaving in two days," Ray answered. "Great! I'm supposed to be meeting my group here in a few minutes. We are going to be transported to base camp. I'm hoping to start the climb tomorrow."

"Tomorrow? You done much climbing before?" Ray asked.

"No. Too busy. But, I've always wanted to beat Everest. I'm a fast study. That's why I run the best plastic surgery clinic in L.A.," the man boasted.

He flashed a movie-star smile. Ray thought he looked like he was auditioning to be the next James Bond. Just then, a van pulled up and a group of rugged, muscular climbers got out.

"You Parker Frost?" a bearded man asked Ray.

Before he could answer, the plastic surgeon was shoving Ray aside and extending his million-dollar hand.

"I'm Parker Frost. Pleasure to meet you."

The bearded man rolled his eyes and sighed. Ray hung back, observing the exchange of introductions.

Parker sauntered back inside the hotel lobby and returned moments later leading a harassed bellhop with a cart of what looked like brand-new gear.

Ray looked in the back of the van. The gear already stowed there looked aged, but well taken care of. It had grit to it. Parker's gear gleamed by comparison. Ray watched as the gear was loaded up and as the van pulled away.

Two days passed, and Ray was standing back outside the hotel with a pile of his own gritty gear. The van pulled up and the same bearded man from before greeted him.

"You Ray Alphonse?"

"That's me," Ray said. Ray helped the man pack his gear while a handful of other climbers stretched their legs.

The bearded man slammed shut the back doors to the van. Ray and the other passengers got in the van and headed out of town.

Later at base camp, Ray couldn't help but smile as he looked around. He had found his climbing group easily. He had met most of them on his different treks training for this very moment. He spent the days mostly going over routes, packing and repacking his stuff, and getting used to the thin air. Looming in the backdrop of his preparation was Everest.

Over the next several days, he and his group made their way to camps higher and higher to the top. Ray couldn't believe how big it was. Even at base camp it still seemed impossibly tall. *No, not impossibly,* Ray thought, correcting his initial impression of the giant mountain. *Just tall.* He was ready for this. Tomorrow, the start of their attack of the mountain would mark 10 years exactly from the day his sister slid into death the same way he slid into a summer afternoon nap.

On the morning of the final ascent, Ray was filled with nervous energy. He forced himself to avoid needless walking and movement. He wanted to conserve his energy to submit to the rigors of the climb.

Nobody but the Sherpa spoke as they headed out of camp. They had been out two hours when the Sherpa motioned for them to stop. He motioned to a flag. Flags of its kind marked the scene of a dead body.

"This is the newest body on the mountain. Most don't die this low, where the climb is so easy," the Sherpa said matter-of-factly.

Ray stared at the body—thinking about his sister, their parents, and her kids. He knew he carried all their hopes with him for a successful climb. He knew he couldn't fail.

He was about to look away when he noticed something

at the base of the flag. It was an expensive gold watch—just like the one Parker had worn several days before.

The Sherpa saw Ray looking at the watch. "Some rich fool tried to bribe his way to an early ascent. Said he was a fast learner. Rumor is he bribed another guide with that watch. But, the man was not acclimated. He died right here. Just fell over. The guide felt so guilty about taking the bribe, he left the watch. Probably just a rumor. Time to go."

Everyone except Ray laughed at the dead idiot. Ray used the spare moment to check his gear again. He figured the only difference between him and a dead body on the mountain was preparation.

For Your Consideration

Read the questions below, then answer them completely and transparently.

1. Whose preparation was the most beneficial?
2. What supports your decision?
3. How would you end this story?

MEDITATE ON THIS

Write the following quotation and Scripture in a journal. Then provide critical thinking about each one and write how each one speaks to you. That is, how is each one renewing your mindset when it comes to your fulfillment for living and spirituality?

Quotation

The time to repair the roof is when the sun is shining.
— John F. Kennedy

Scripture

And having shod your feet with the preparation of the gospel of peace.
Ephesians 6:15

SELF-ASSESSMENT

Answer each question fully and to the best of your ability. Remember, because there is no judgment or wrong answers in whatever you write, strive to be transparent.

1. What is your perspective on being prepared? Have you ever felt unprepared and if so, how did it feel?

   _____
   _____
   _____
   _____

2. Whom have you helped prepare for success?

   _____
   _____
   _____
   _____

3. How does it feel to know you are prepared for whatever happens?

   _____
   _____
   _____
   _____

4. Who helps you prepare for whatever you have to face?

   _____
   _____
   _____
   _____

TAKE ACTION

1. I will do the following to be better prepared every day.

    _____

    _____

    _____

    _____

2. I will remove the following obstacles that hinder me from being prepared.

    _____

    _____

    _____

    _____

3. For which major event(s), if any, are you currently trying to prepare?

    _____

    _____

    _____

    _____

HUMILITY

If there is one thing I have learned on this incredible journey we call life, it is this: the sign of a truly successful individual is humility.

Naveen Jain

HU·MIL·I·TY

a modest or low view of one's own importance

2

Recently, social media platforms were all abuzz with pictures and stories of a former TV star who was spotted bagging groceries at one of the locations of a national grocer. Many who caught the story felt the person 'job-shaming' the former star did so to embarrass him. It might have worked, too, had it not been for the former actor's own humility. When asked about being outed as a grocery store worker, the former star humbly responded, "work is work." No ducking the situation. No pretending the job as a bagger wasn't his. This actor bravely and humbly admitted he was indeed happily working a position that many individuals would consider a step down from his television days on a popular sit-com. The actor's humility in embracing the deliberate job-shaming culminated in several undeniable blessings. First, in the midst of all the drama over his lowly employment, a plethora of international support as well as numerous job offers rolled in, most notably from a famous Hollywood producer. Then, on the heels of the employment opportunities and verbal affirmations, a notable entertainer promised a sizable donation toward his living expenses. All in all, the outcome to the job-shaming wasn't bad, thanks to this actor's humble reaction to a seemingly mean-spirited motive to humiliate him.

Just so we're clear, humility is not synonymous to weakness or cowardice. On the contrary, *it takes a lot of strength and courage* to take the high road when your circumstances or situation provokes you to answer evil with evil. Additionally, humility does not mean putting yourself down just to make someone else look good or being a doormat. Self-degradation and humility are not counterparts. They are opposites. In the case of self-degradation, one fails to see his/her self-worth and honor, while a person of humility always possesses self-value and honor, irrespective of his/her environment or circumstances. With that said, let us take a deeper dive into humility to see why it's one of those words that should be passed on.

Success and Humility, a Perfect Bond

Being knowledgeable alone is not the secret to success. Neither is just having a lot of money. Many people possess both and still are not content or fulfilled, which is why they stay on the hunt for the latest this or the newest that to make them satisfied. Success was not meant to be some impossible-to-reach goal that you chase down all your life. It is possible to have life-long fulfillment, but first, you must be willing to go low for it. Here's what we mean.

Believe it or not, humility is the secret to success and fulfillment. Yet interestingly, humility is an attribute that schools, colleges and universities must teach alongside the core subjects of education. That means reading and arithmetic are no longer enough to make for good learners. Learning institutions are discovering more and more that their young constituents are coming to them without attributes that positively mold a person's character. They know many other things, like the latest fashion, music, lyrics to a newly-produced CD, who's been drafted onto professional sports teams, and so on. What they lack is character. And, as previously mentioned, humility is one of them. This is an unfortunate circumstance because humility is the one attribute, we think, that grows success. Naturally you ask, "Why is that?" Because it keeps a person from becoming overconfident, thereby impeding their progress. Those successes could include health, wealth and life-long relationships—things we all need for fulfillment.

Here is something else to think about when it comes

pairing humility with success. At some point, individuals who feel they have leadership potential quite naturally want to lead others. The problem is this: if the one leading has a propensity to be more prideful and egotistical than humble, then fewer people will want to follow. Employers are well aware of this and quite naturally tend to withhold leadership opportunities from those individuals overly confident of themselves. They know such individuals inherently lack courtesy, respect for others, an inability to compromise, and other qualities that help grow individual success or that of a business rather than destroy it. Sadly, people who lack humility inadvertently prevent the growth of their own success. And, limited success could equal limited fulfillment.

One final thought before we move on to a story about humility. If you ever want to experience the feeling of self-assurance, humble yourself. Then redirect your thoughts to more positive and influential activities.

A Story about Humility

If there was one thing that Jim hated, it was fishing. He hated getting up early in the morning. He hated heading out into the middle of nowhere. What he hated most was all of the waiting he had to do before he caught anything.

But, here Jim was, in the truck with his grandpa, heading out to some secret fishing spot before the sun was even up over the horizon.

Jim was only going because his parents had pressured him to go. Somehow, they were sure Papa James would be able to help him figure out what to do. It was a sign of both how much Jim loved his parents and how desperate he was that he had agreed to go.

Papa James had always been kind to Jim. In many ways he was the perfect grandfather. He was always up for anything the grandkids wanted to do, even if it was a water fight. But, as Jim had gotten older, he had started to notice something about his grandpa that bothered him.

Papa James was always asking other people what he should do. When he was ordering food, he always asked the server what to order. When the car had a flat tire, he would ask everyone in the car what he should do. It seemed to him that his grandpa, while always kind, was incapable of making even the smallest decision without input from others.

In contrast, Jim hated getting input from other people. He figured he was just as smart as the next guy, and that nobody else understood his life as well as he did. Papa James led an incredible life. He was a decorated soldier. Even though Papa James would never tell the story, Jim had learned that his grandfather had charged an enemy installation by himself to capture an enemy artillery piece that was shelling his men.

26

Papa James started his own business, a business that Jim's father now runs, and that Jim had worked at since he was a teenager. People at the office told crazy stories about Papa James, how skilled a businessman he was, and the risk he had taken.

Jim couldn't see how that man was the same one who asked his wife what shirts he should buy when they went shopping. Had he just burned out from making too many decisions? Jim was having trouble of his own with a decision for the first time in his life. He had asked everyone he respected what he should do but didn't feel any closer to an answer. When he finished college next month, should he go back to work at the family business, or should he accept the scholarship he had received for graduate school? Jim couldn't figure out the best thing to do.

The truck went over a bump and Jim pulled out of his stupor. "Did I wake you up with that last one?" Papa James chuckled. Jim smiled. "No, I was awake. I've just been thinking."

"Dangerous." "What's dangerous?"

"Thinking," Papa James said. He looked over at Jim and winked.

"You're liable to make a decision if you think too much." The truck slowed at a fork in the road.

"Well, what do you think Jim? Left to the lake or right towards where the river starts to feed into the lake?"

Before Jim knew what was happening, the question he had held inside for most of his young life came spilling out.

"Papa, why do you always ask everyone else to tell you what you should do? Why don't you just make your own decisions?"

The booming sound of Papa James's laughter filled the truck.

"Is that what this fishing trip is about? You just wanted to ask me about my love of asking questions?"

"I'm sorry. I didn't mean to be rude. I'm just stressed about my own inability to make a single decision." Jim said.

"I learned a long time ago that by asking others to share their knowledge, experience, and opinions I became wiser and made fewer mistakes."

"Why ask me about which road to take? I've never been here, and I don't even really know anything about fishing." Jim said.

"True. But, I care more about spending time with you than I do about where we end up. I asked you because if you had a preference, I would rather make you happy than just make a decision about something inconsequential." Papa James said.

It suddenly became clear to Jim why his parents had been so insistent that he talk to Papa James. What Jim had taken for indecisiveness on the part of his grandpa was really humility and wisdom. Jim shared his dilemma with Papa James and for the first time in his young life, he listened intently to someone else's opinion.

For Your Consideration

Answer the following questions as truthfully and transparently as you can.

When was the last time you mistook someone's humility for indecisiveness? What did you do to correct your opinion about this person?

MEDITATE ON THIS

Write the following quotation and Scripture in a journal. Then provide critical thinking about each one and write how each one speaks to you. That is, how is each one renewing your mindset when it comes to your fulfillment for living and spirituality?

Quotation

It takes guts and humility to admit mistakes. Admitting we're wrong is courage, not weakness.
— Roy T. Bennett

Scripture

Let nothing be done through selfish ambition or conceit, but in lowliness of mind let each esteem others better than himself.
Philippians 2:3

Self-Assessment

Answer each question fully and to the best of your ability. Remember, because there is no judgment in whatever you write, strive to be transparent.

1. What are some strong characteristics of humility? What are some negative characteristics of humility?

   _____

   _____

   _____

   _____

2. Explain why some people think there is such a thing as being too humble.

   _____

   _____

   _____

   _____

3. Describe someone who is humble.

   _____

   _____

   _____

   _____

4. On a scale of 1 to 5 (with 5 being the humblest, and 1 the least humble), rate your own level of humility. Explain your results.

   _____

   _____

   _____

   _____

TAKE ACTION

1. I will encourage humility in others by

   _____
   _____
   _____
   _____

2. Describe three situations where you could have shown more humility and how it would have made a difference.

   _____
   _____
   _____
   _____

COURAGE

Courage is what it takes to stand up and speak.
Courage is also what it takes to sit down and listen.

Winston Churchill

Cour·Age

the ability to do something that frightens people;
strength in the face of pain or grief

3

D ream big. That's the going advice lately for individuals wanting to become, say, entrepreneurs. The thought behind the advice is that once you dream big, then it is encumbered upon you to make it happen—almost like magic. Well, dreaming big is not the problem. In fact, it's probably not that hard to do once you get started. The problem is getting the courage to move that dream from an idea on paper to reality. It's what our Jewish brothers and sisters call *hutzpah*, the shameless, gutsy nerve to bust a move. The point is this: at some point during our lifetime, we must factor in courage if we ever expect to live a fulfilled, contented life. Simply put, there is less contentment without courage.

Courage and Contentment
—A Necessary Relationship for Fulfilled Living

Pure and simple, courage equals contentment, though being content is not always easy. Let's face it, you could be experiencing the most depressing moment in your life while others around you are giddy and content, completely oblivious to your misery. Yet, the fact remains that contentment is available to every one of us, regardless of what we may feel. Here's why.

Being content is a choice. It's the way you think about your circumstances, your purpose, the present, the future, even your past with its mixture of frustrations, mistakes and good times. The daunting task is to push back the cynicism and make a deliberate effort to see things differently, and in most cases to do things differently. Sometimes this means making the choice to change friends with whom you normally socialize. For example, suppose you and some friends thought it entertaining to gossip about others and put them down to make up for your own insecurities. However, your insecurities linger, and the put-downs only leave you feeling empty and miserable. Though you are fond of these friends, you know without a doubt that you need to drop them and surround yourself with people who encourage others and see things through a positive lens. Your sense of contentment depends on your making this change. This is where courage comes into play because letting go of friends (even ones that are not good for you is not always easy. Courage is what it takes to send them on their way and empower you to find new ones. If this example fits you at all, I want you to rest in this: you *do* have the courage to let go of what is not good for you and replace it with people and things that are. You have the courage to explore new opportunities, including making new friends who do not waste life with negative thinking. Reach inside. Your courage is there.

Courage and Destiny

You cannot find purpose without courage. In the first place, courage is the fuel that helps us identify our destiny and pursue it with all we've got. The 'why' of our existence does not come easily for some of us. Which means we have to summon the courage to do what is necessary to answer the age-old question, "Why am I here?". As Robert Frost suggests in his poem, "The Road Not Taken," this journey to discovering purpose may put us on unexpected paths. To be honest, facing crossroads can be intimidating. In this case, courage is that one quality that helps us face down the fear that comes with making decisions about the unknown. The journey to discovery, Frost suggests, is not an easy one, but a necessary one if we expect to discover and live out our intended purpose. On this, we couldn't agree more. The Word of God expressly says the Lord Himself has planned out our lives (Jeremiah 29:11 and that His plans lead to a fulfilled life, which He expresses as "a hope and a future." It takes courage to actively find out His plans and pursue them.

Pass this on—by all accounts it's courage which undergirds fulfilled, contented, purposeful living. And, we believe courage is a quality we all have. It does not have to be bought or made up. It resides within each of us and can be summoned at any time.

A STORY ON COURAGE

Sheila was excited to be starting high school. Middle school had been rough at times, but she emerged with a core group of friends. She had finally grown into her body. She no longer tripped over her own feet. On the basketball court, she had found talent that she never knew she had and positive attention she never knew was possible. She noticed that her classmates were nicer to her now. She just felt like everything was somehow easier.

During her first week of high school, Sheila made new friends every day. She quickly realized that she was now one of the popular girls. People stared at her, but not in disgust as they once had. Instead, Sheila thought that maybe some people were actually jealous of her.

After the second week, things were going better than ever. Her classes were not as hard as she had expected. Basketball tryouts had gone so well, that she had made the varsity team as a freshman—something Coach Lamb said he had never before allowed.

But, during the third week of school, Sheila began to have some worries. She noticed that at lunch while she and her new friends were laughing, there was a girl just a few tables over that always sat alone. It looked like she had a force field around her. Nobody ever got near her. Sheila even noticed that people would rather sit on the floor against the wall, rather than sit by the lonely girl.

Sheila had asked her friends the girl's name. They laughed. They told her that girl was "special" and not worth anyone's time. Then one of her new friends asked Sheila menacingly, "Why do you care about her?"

Sheila didn't know what to say. She suddenly felt vulnerable and meekly responded, "Just curious."

Every day Sheila watched the girl at the other table, hoping someone would sit by her, but no one ever did. Sheila quickly felt her elation at being popular fade. Every time she asked about the lonely girl, her friends teased her or ignored her. She once even suggested they all go sit by the girl, or at least ask her name. Her friends laughed so loud at that idea that a teacher had come over to tell them to settle down.

After six weeks of being in high school, Sheila noticed that every day at lunch was the same. Sheila found that she couldn't help staring at the girl. But, the more she stared, the sicker she felt. She should have been happy. She was now a starter on the varsity basketball team. Her team was undefeated. Coach Lamb had talked to her parents about what they could do to prepare her for college. He thought that she might be able to get a full scholarship. But Sheila was miserable. It even started to affect her ability to study. She couldn't stop thinking about the lonely girl. It was getting close to Thanksgiving. Sheila realized she couldn't bear to go on break thinking about the girl at the lunch table. She hadn't even bothered to learn the girl's name yet.

Sheila made a decision. The next lunch period she would make her move, no matter what the consequences were. The worst part was the walk over to the table. Once Sheila passed the table where she usually sat at with her friends, she felt the eyes of everyone in the cafeteria on her. She felt tightness in her chest that wouldn't go away even when she remembered to take a deep breath and exhale. It was only a few extra feet to the table where the special girl sat by herself, her head down, eating her paper bag lunch. Once she got to the table, she set her tray down across the table and spoke, barely above a whisper. She asked, "Can I sit with you?"

The girl looked up at Sheila in shock. "Sure," she said.

"My name is Sheila. What's yours?"

The girl eyed Sheila warily, waiting for the punchline. Sheila sat down and began eating her lunch. The cafeteria seemed unusually quiet. She could see some of her friends pointing and laughing. Others were trying not to look at her at all.

"My name is Tammy," the girl finally said. Sheila smiled. "Why are you sitting by me?"

"Well, Tammy, I am looking for some new friends."

Tammy smiled and kept eating. Sheila felt a surge of happiness. She felt like a huge weight had been lifted off her chest. The noise of the cafeteria gradually picked up and Sheila's old friends got tired of pointing at her. Sheila was finally excited about school again.

For Your Consideration

Use the space available to answer the question as truthfully and transparently as you can.

What causes you to struggle with being courageous? How do you overcome the struggle?

SELF-ASSESSMENT

Answer each question fully and to the best of your ability. Remember, because there is no judgment or wrong answers in whatever you write, strive to be transparent.

1. How is it possible to pass courage on to someone else without losing your own?

   _____

   _____

   _____

   _____

2. Recall the last time you used courage in the face of fear.

   _____

   _____

   _____

   _____

TAKE ACTION

1. The next two courageous moments for me will be to

   _____

   _____

   _____

   _____

2. I will inspire courage in others by

   _____

   _____

   _____

   _____

3. I will not let the following fears get in the way of my being courageous.

   _____

   _____

   _____

   _____

LOVE

Love keeps no record of wrongs.

I Corinthians 13:5

LOVE

an intense feeling of deep affection

4

Is this how you love? Measure your love against the love you see here.

Love is patient, love is kind. It does not envy, it does not boast, it is not proud. It does not dishonor others, it is not self-seeking, it is not easily angered, it keeps no record of wrongs. Love does not delight in evil but rejoices with the truth. It always protects, always trusts, always hopes, always perseveres. Love never fails.

1 Corinthians 13:4-8a

A popular song in the late eighties asked the question, "What's love got to do with it?" Apparently, a lot, according to God's Word. God's perspective is that love is the answer to anything life throws at us—from being hated to being loved back. From what we can tell from these verses, God expects us to handle everything in life with love; that is, His kind of love, which is the highest, purest form of love there is. It's the kind of love that is easy to receive, but difficult to give. Nevertheless, it is the standard of God; therefore, it is not impossible to act on, for He gives us nothing that we cannot bear. Earlier, we told you that passing on positive, encouraging words is transformational and necessary to your life journey, which includes spiritual growth. We still stand by that. For the purposes of this chapter, we will spend time influencing your spiritual growth by transforming your mind on how you presently think about love. We believe that love is from God. Therefore, love is a spiritual matter of the heart and should be defined by the One who created it and gave it to us to share with one another. With that said, let's begin to unpack love in many of its iterations as delineated by God Himself.

Love is Patient and Kind

Love puts up with stuff—all kinds of stuff because it's relentless. It carries the quality of perseverance. That means no matter the insult or personal injury, love can still triumph. Here's how: love does not push back with pain. Instead, it answers hurts of all variations and degrees with acts of kindness. This is why love is also kind.

One of the greatest examples of enduring love is the sacrificial passion of Christ. Many point to His death on the cross as His greatest act of love. We don't deny that, but before the cross came the beatings with multiple lashes. Each lash ripped open His skin and exposed the flesh and sent our Christ into gut-wrenching pain. If you think the Son of God did not cry out, think again. Those lashes were painful. Of course He responded with screams from the pain. That brutal beating was meant to kill Him, but His relentless love endured the repeated strikes to His back, legs, and thighs. Not once did His love speak, "Stop."

Like love, kindness overlooks wrongs. That does not mean you will not battle with withholding favor when you were the one who was wronged. Naturally in cases of wrongdoing, anger rises and demands a clapback your wrongdoer will never forget. Counter the demand instead by doing something good for that person. Surprise the one who hurt you deeply with a deliberate act of kindness.

Love's Qualities of Modesty, Honor, Generosity, Hope, and Self-Restraint

Have you ever caught yourself saying "serves him right" when someone who is not happy for you was publicly exposed for some mistake? Do you refuse to pray for elected officials whose politics are different from yours? Do you hope the best for them, or do you harbor a desire to see them fail and get tossed out of office?

What about people you come across who believe differently than you? Do you find yourself wishing them good or evil? Do you go out of your way to make sure you never say anything more than "hello" to them? How do you handle disagreements with your spouse, relatives, friends and enemies? Do you tend to shut down at their suggestions and ideas when they're better than yours? And, for those who seem to get away with just about everything, what do you wish for them? Blessings or curses?

In each of these hypothetical situations, love is not to be suppressed. God's expectation is that you extend it with no consideration whatsoever of the demographics of the one receiving it or the circumstances under which you show love. In fact, God's Word insists that you love others as you love yourself, which makes a lot of sense. After all, until you love yourself, it would be difficult for you to extend this emotion to anyone else. Nothing matters except that you give love.

Admittedly, showing the qualities of love no matter what the circumstance is not easy. In fact, it may be the hardest challenge that any of us can ever achieve. But here's the thing: we are all called to love. And, we are called to love the way God intended. It's the kind of love where everyone involved benefits and no one gets hurts.

Love Forgives Because It Keeps No Records

To people who think that they are justified in a persistently unforgiving attitude toward someone who has hurt them, we want to make this perfectly clear: your unforgiveness is not justified. It is not excused, dear friend. And, you are in the wrong if you persist in it. You should know that your spiritual growth is contingent upon your willingness to forgive.

Along with extending forgiveness, love challenges you to do away with the mental recordkeeping of who did what to you once and for all. Refuse to allow your mind to linger in places where you were hurt. Instead, replace those bad memories by creating positive ones where you are returning love for hurt. Now, this does not mean that you make yourself a doormat for anyone just to prove how forgiving you are. Wisdom, too, must still be at the heart of what you do. What we are saying is that you must take conscious, deliberate steps toward the love you were intended to show.

We don't have a fancy or dramatic ending to this chapter. What we have is a sincere request that you pay it forward with love because it is the only thing to which hatred itself succumbs. Every time.

A Love Story

Ray stepped inside his empty house, filled his lungs with the cool air, and then exhaled loudly. He dropped his duffle bag and kicked off his shoes. He walked over to the couch and fell backwards on it. Ray stretched out his aching limbs.

Last away shift for a while, Ray thought to himself as a grin slowly spread across his face. He had been on duty at a remote worksite for the past two weeks. He had been awake for the past forty-some hours.

Ray's muscles began to relax as he heard the hum of the air conditioner. He closed his eyes and almost fell asleep. His pocket buzzed. Ray shook his head awake and pulled out his phone. There was a calendar alert on the screen. It was a single word. Anniversary. Ray sat up in a panic. *Today? I thought it was tomorrow!*

He checked the date again on his phone. It was today. His phone buzzed again.

"Ray, you make it home yet? Happy anniversary. Wish I could be there today to welcome you home!"

Ray tapped back. "Just got in. Happy anniversary to you, too! I love you."

Ray saw that his wife was typing another message.

"Get some sleep. You must be exhausted. I'm volunteering in Maya's class all day today. We'll see you this afternoon ... or tonight. Whenever you wake up. I love you, too."

Ray smiled and thought to himself, "How'd I get so lucky?" The panic of not remembering to get a present faded. She would understand; she always did. He went into the bedroom, ready to follow her orders and go to sleep.

The bed was a mess. A flash of irritation came as he spotted Maya's stuffed pink elephant and pillow. He also noticed a lot of tissues and a bottle of cough syrup on the headboard. The irritation fled.

It must have been a rough time around here.

Ray picked up the tissues and put away the cough syrup. He stripped the bed and gathered Maya's belongings. He walked upstairs to her room. He stripped her bed, too.

He went to the linen closet and hunted around for some sheets. Seconds later he pulled out a fresh set for his bed and for Maya's. As he began making Maya's bed, all his exhaustion fled. Before leaving Maya's room, he placed her pillow and her elephant on top of the perfectly tucked in bedspread.

Ray headed downstairs to his own room. He quickly made his soft, king-sized bed and was momentarily tempted to just get some sleep. But then he thought of Christine lying in bed all night with Maya, and pushed the temptation away.

After making the bed, he grabbed all the dirty sheets and headed to the laundry room. There was a load in the washer and the dryer. Ray smiled again. He switched the laundry, carefully folding the clothes in the dryer. Once he got the dryer and washer started with their new loads, he took the folded laundry and put them away.

Next, Ray headed into the kitchen. Just as he expected, the breakfast dishes were all still out. He unloaded the dishwasher, filled it back up with the breakfast dishes, and cleaned the counters. While cleaning off the kitchen table he noticed the remains of three or four meals on top of the floor, under the edge of the table. Ray swept and mopped the entire kitchen. Ray smiled again. He wasn't sure if he was happy or just delirious. He decided he was probably a bit of both.

Ray went back into the front of the house. He cleaned up his shoes and duffle bag. Then he went room to room, vacuuming, dusting, and picking up.

Ray checked the clock. School would be out in 90 minutes. Ray thought he had just enough time to clean the bathrooms. He started to hum as he worked at getting toilets to sparkle. He laughed when he realized he was humming the theme song to his daughter's favorite cartoon.

After he finished the bathroom, Ray took a shower. He made sure to clean up after himself in the bathroom. He checked the time again. School would be out in ten minutes. Ray decided to sit in his recliner and wait for everyone to get home. The moment Ray got into the chair, his eyes closed involuntarily, and he fell into a deep sleep. After some time, Ray opened his eyes. He had to blink several times. It was dark. It took him a moment to remember where he was. *I'm at home in my chair*, he said to himself. He stood up. It was after 11:00 at night. He had been asleep for nine hours. He felt another stab of panic. *My anniversary*, he thought. Then, he walked back into his bedroom. Christine was lying there looking at her phone.

She smiled when she spotted Ray in the doorway.

"Look who's awake!" Ray said laughing. "I'm so sorry, Christine."

"For what?"

"For falling asleep. I wanted to see you and Maya. I'm sorry for not giving you a better anniversary."

Christine started to cry.

Ray felt a lump in his own throat. How can I possibly let this woman down yet again? I don't deserve her. She is always picking up the slack for me. Ray moved towards the bed.

Christine said, "Ray, you gave me the most amazing anniversary gift. You cleaned everything. You even made our bed. I know you hate making the bed."

Ray sighed. He got in bed and wrapped his arms around Christine.

"There was no better way for you to tell me that you loved me than to clean like you did, when you were so tired after working so hard for our family. I love you, Raymond Dean Stephenson."

Ray let the tears fall from his eyes. He held Christine as tightly as he could without hurting her.

"Thanks for letting me sleep. I needed that. You always know what I need." It was all Ray could say.

He and Christine sat there holding each other, crying, until they fell asleep.

For Your Consideration

Use the space below to answer the question with truth and transparency.

In your opinion, how difficult is it to love the way prescribed in 1 Corinthians 13? Explain whether this is a realistic way to love.

MEDITATE ON THIS

Write the following quotation and Scripture in a journal. Then critically think about each one and write how each one speaks to you. That is, how is each one renewing your mindset on the principle of loving being key to your fulfillment in life and spirituality?

Quotation

> *Piglet: "How do you spell 'love'?"*
> *Pooh: "You don't spell it... you feel it."*
> *—A.A. Milne*

Scripture

And now abide faith, hope, love, these three; but the greatest of these is love.
1 Corinthians 13:13

SELF-ASSESSMENT

Answer each question fully and to the best of your ability. Remember, because there is no judgment in whatever you write, strive to be transparent.

1. How do you express your love?

   _____
   _____
   _____
   _____

2. How do you know that you are loved?

   _____
   _____
   _____
   _____

3. List the people who you believe see love through you.

   _____
   _____
   _____
   _____

4. Explain why love is a necessity to your spiritual growth, fulfillment and purpose in life.

   _____
   _____
   _____
   _____

TAKE ACTION

1. I will show the following random acts of kindness in 21 days or less.

    _____

    _____

    _____

    _____

2. I will do the following to show at least three others that I love them. Be sure to name the three people.

    _____

    _____

    _____

    _____

3. I will take the following steps to love myself more.

    _____

    _____

    _____

    _____

SERVICE

To give real service you must add something which cannot be bought or measured with money, and that is sincerity and integrity.

Douglas Adams

SER·VICE

contributions to the welfare of others

5

Our culture is dominated by this one thought: "What's in it for me?" More than anything, financial incentives are the driving force behind some people's decision to return a service with a service. But to be clear, that's not serving; that's just working to get paid. As our definition suggests, serving is about character. And character is a mindset and matter of the heart, which makes service all about how one thinks and feels he should contribute to the life of another person.

Attitude is everything. If we want to serve, then we have to do so with the heart, which entails transforming our minds from a culture of "me" to "us". We realize this is easier said than done, so we'd like to offer some considerations that may compel you to adopt a service mindset as part of your lifestyle.

First, consider this: you have a range of resources at your disposal that are of great benefit to others; take time, for instance. This is one of the most valuable assets. You can serve your own community by donating a few hours of your life a month, quarter or year through volunteerism. You can donate blood, collect and distribute needed items after a natural disaster has devastated your area, or even adopt a highway and help keep it clean. There are so many things your community needs to help it thrive. If you want to help, contact some non-profit organizations in your area. They are almost always understaffed and under-resourced. The time you give them will invariably make a difference to how much they are able to keep the community thriving. This brings us to the next point.

Service helps improve the quality of life. Not just your own, but someone else's, and here's how. Sometimes offering service to others provides an opportunity to develop new skills or build on existing experiences and knowledge. Help implies furnishing anything that furthers one's efforts or relieve another's wants or necessities. For example, recently, our editor and her state faced a devastating hurricane, perhaps the worst in American history. At any rate, other people not affected rallied to their rescue by donating packs and packs of water, food, housing and even money to replace lost funds—all to improve the quality of life in the midst of a disaster. Then there is Habitat for Humanity, where the mission is to build affordable housing all through volunteerism of people's time, building supplies and skills. As of November 2013, Habitat for Humanity has built 800,000 homes. In case you missed it, that's 800,000 families whose quality of life has been improved by the service of others.

Here's the point about service: as you move from a "me" orientation to a "we" orientation, you will realize that it's not receiving some sort of payment that satisfies. It's other things you have to offer and bring to a life at no cost that really, really matter. Things like your time, attention, talents, skill set, and so on. These are what add to the quality of life for others and will bring the greatest satisfaction to them as well as yourself. Then, ask yourself, "How long will I continue to wait to change the world?". You're needed now! If this does not convince you of the value of service, look below at the results that service brings[1].

- It lowers rates of depression and puts you in a better mood.

- It lowers your risk of dying by at least 22%.

---

[1] Retrieved from the internet
http://dosomethingcool.net/helping- others-life/www.dosomethingcool.net/helping-others-life/
September 21, 2018, 10:43PM.

- It's good for your mental health.

Serve however you want, but serve, without attention or fame. Otherwise, that's not serving; that's being served. The world defines greatness in terms of power, possessions and position. However, Jesus measures greatness in terms of service, not status. It's our deepest belief that God determines greatness in terms of how many you serve, not how many serve you. This is because *your growth and success are determined by the growth, success and welfare of those you serve.*

A STORY ABOUT SERVICE

Jack didn't want to go see Mr. Dawson. Ever since they moved to the neighborhood, his mom made him go with her every Saturday to read to Mr. Dawson. It made Jack uncomfortable. His mother said Mr. Dawson was the same age as she was. But he seemed much older. He was mostly bald with gray patches of hair on the sides. His skin was baggy. He smelled. He sat all day in his chair. His hands moved strangely. He mumbled. The guy just gave Jack the creeps.

Nevertheless, every week, Jack and his mom would go walk down to the Dawson's house and ring the doorbell. Mrs. Dawson would answer the door and escort them into Mr. Dawson's sitting room. Then she would leave while Jack and his mom took turns reading some book to Mr. Dawson. Jack thought it was weird how Mrs. Dawson always looked like she was about to cry. He also hated how it seemed like Mr. Dawson never paid attention when they read to him, which he and his mom had been doing weekly for three years.

Jack was 13. He realized that Mr. Dawson had cerebral palsy. His mind was fine, but his body rebelled against him.

Jack still didn't enjoy the weekly reading sessions. He hated having to wait until he could play with his friends, but he knew it was important to his mom. By now he had gotten used to the smell and the funny way Mr. Dawson's body moved. He even thought he could see happiness in Mr. Dawson's eyes when they started reading. It seemed that Mr. Dawson liked the books about pirates and ocean battles the best. Or, maybe Jack just liked those books best.

As time wore on, Jack noticed that the Dawson's yard was becoming more and more of a mess. He also thought that Mrs. Dawson looked like she was stooping more and more. Like Mr.

Dawson, she now looked much older than his mother, even though they were all about the same age.

One Saturday after they had finished reading, Jack surprised himself and his mom by asking if he could start mowing the Dawson's lawn after they read. When Jack told his mom he didn't want to do it for money, he thought he saw a tear in the corner of her eye.

Grown-ups were a mystery to Jack. But, he started mowing the lawn regularly. Sometimes he would also spend time pulling weeds and trimming the trees. Under Jack's careful care, the Dawson's yard returned to looking respectable in just a few short weeks.

One Friday evening, the doorbell rang. His mom answered the door and Jack, who had recently turned 14, heard Mrs. Dawson mumbling something. He came around the corner to find his mom hugging Mrs. Dawson. They were both crying.

There was no reading the next day. There was no mowing the lawn, either. A week later Jack and his mom attended Mr. Dawson's funeral.

There weren't many people there. Mr. Dawson's older brother was there and said a few words. Mrs. Dawson sat by Jack and his mom. The only other people in attendance were the few people who worked at the funeral home.

After the funeral, Jack returned to mowing the Dawson's lawn and did so for the rest of his teen years. One hot summer day, Mrs. Dawson came out to watch him. She had a pitcher of cool lemonade. After the grass was cut, she offered Jack a glass and they talked a while. She told him she was selling the house. Thanks to his work on the yard, the house sold for more than she ever thought possible. She was going to move into a retirement community. She told Jack she wanted to thank him. She explained that he would never understand what his and his mom's service had meant to her and to Mr. Dawson.

Jack felt embarrassed. He thanked Mrs. Dawson and wished her the best. She moved out of the neighborhood the next week, and he never saw her again. He went off to college, got a job across the country, married and had a couple of children.

One weekend, Jack was back home visiting his mom with his family. He heard his mom stirring in the early hours on a Saturday morning. He went down to find her getting ready to go out. When he asked her what she was doing, his mom explained she went every Saturday to read to a woman from church. The woman was blind and bedridden. She was also expected to die very soon. When Jack heard that, he asked his mom to wait so he could read with her. His mom smiled and asked him if he knew why she spent as many Saturdays as possible reading to the sick.

Jack had no idea.

His mom explained that as a young woman she had found books to be a great way to escape from the stresses of life. Shortly after she had gotten married to Jack's father, she got pregnant with Jack. It was a tough pregnancy that put her on mandatory bed rest for much of the time. Jack's dad would spend every night reading to her as she sat in bed. It helped her escape but still feel loved and connected.

On the day Jack was born, his dad was killed in a car accident as he left the hospital to go home to find a new book to read to his wife in the hospital.

By reading to others, Jack's mom felt that she was passing on the love Jack's father had felt for her to others by reading to them and keeping them company.

Jack felt his eyes begin to water. When he and his family returned home, Jack found that there was a woman with cerebral palsy not too far from his home. One Saturday, he and his oldest daughter took a book and went to read to her.

For Your Consideration

Use the space below to answer the question with as much truth and transparency as you can.

How would you measure your service to others?

MEDITATE ON THIS

Write the following quotation and Scripture in a journal. Then critically think about each one and write how each one speaks to you. That is, how is each one renewing your mindset on the principle of service being key to your fulfillment in life and spirituality?

Quotation

Your own Self-Realization is the greatest service you can render the world.
—Ramana Maharshi

Scripture

With goodwill doing service, as to the Lord, and not to men.
Ephesians 6:7

SELF-ASSESSMENT

Answer each question fully and to the best of your ability. Remember, because there are no judgments or wrong answers in whatever you write, strive to be transparent.

1. How can service to others be fulfilling?

   _____
   _____
   _____
   _____

2. What are some benefits of going from a self-serving mindset to a servant mindset?

   _____
   _____
   _____
   _____

TAKE ACTION

1. How can I better serve others?

   _____

   _____

   _____

   _____

2. I will promote the importance of service by

   _____

   _____

   _____

   _____

3. If I do

   _____

   _____

   _____

   _____

   then I will make a difference on

   _____

   _____

   _____

   _____

COLLABORATION

Alone we can do so little; together we can do so much.

Helen Keller

COL·LAB·O·R A·TION

two or more people working together to achieve or defend a common purpose

6

U sually track and field events wind up with one winner, except in the case of relay team events. Those wind up with four winners instead of one. While individual events call for tremendous speed and skill, the propensity to rely on others for a victorious ending is nowhere because it is not needed. The story is much different for events where the team depends on one thing for a win, and it is not skill. It is collaboration—a joint effort among people to work together to accomplish a common purpose or goal. Without it, the group fails at the task.

The Big Deal about Collaboration

There was once a middle school language arts teacher who assigned facets of a research topic to several groups of students. The teacher deliberately designed the research project in such a way that each group had to depend upon one another to answer the questions. For the groups of students, the goal was to answer all the questions correctly so that their group could get an "A". For their teacher, however, the goal was to teach the importance of collaboration. She knew a 21st Century learning skill her students had to have was the ability to collaborate among others to reach a shared goal. Turns out years later, she was right. Today, her former 7th graders from the 1990s are capable employees who know how to deliver on collaboration at the workplace without becoming disgruntled in the process. Intrinsically, her students were able to adapt several workplace qualities into their culture of learning without feeling certain changes were being rammed down their throats, so to speak. It is not our intention to force anything upon you, either. We do feel, though, that collaboration is such an important quality to have and pass on that we felt compelled to raise its significance in this book. Like the teacher in our story, we feel none of us can do without it.

So, just how is collaboration done? For it to work, there are several elements that must be present, beginning with open communication. Effective communication is the life-blood of a group. It provides every member with equal opportunities to participate and get their ideas across to other members. Of course, this is done with the understanding that everyone must agree to listen to one another, giving each other their full attention. There should be no interrupting one another or tossing in put-downs. From this behavior, we believe an atmosphere of trust among members will be established.

For collaboration to work well, other skills must be in play, from interacting positively with others to using one's manners. Some of the skills include the ability to join in, to commit to working with others, and to speak up with your ideas and opinions clearly and concisely stated as you avoid coming off as opinionated. Also, you have to effectively express your feelings as well as concern for others, without being overbearing. Not to mention it works well when the group has a grasp of common courtesy, such as saying "please", "thank you" and "excuse me".

Finally, nothing blocks a winning collaboration like the refusal to negotiate or compromise. There must be a willingness among members to come to agreements on things. When you cannot agree, then reach for a compromise. Not only is the good of the group at stake, but so is the common purpose, which is something that should not be sacrificed to a stubbornness among group members to come to a mutual understanding. With that said, here's something to pass on: the life-line of the common purpose depends heavily upon the existence of the qualities of collaboration. Without them, the purpose dies as do the relationships among the group members.

A STORY ABOUT COLLABORATION

The Los Angeles-based music scene is notoriously brutal, but Dustin had managed to make a nice career for himself. While nobody outside of the industry knew his name, and only a handful of executives inside the industry knew who he was, Dustin made a nice steady income writing songs that usually ended up in commercials or buried deep on a band's album.

One producer described Dustin's work as eternally proficient, sometimes interesting, but never inspiring. Nobody could deny that Dustin worked hard. He worked on his craft, but he was stuck being a mediocre songwriter.

The truth was that the industry had thousands of artists just like Dustin. Their work was enough to keep them financially independent, but their music never broke out into widespread acclaim.

One day everything changed for Dustin when he met Heidi. Heidi was also an unknown music industry veteran. She and Dustin often competed against each other for gigs for insurance company jingles or coffee commercial soundtracks. They had never met, until they were introduced by a mutual acquaintance at a party. They started talking cautiously at first, like two predators, scoping each other out, but soon they were laughing and talking feverishly. Each sentence the other spoke would trigger a burst of ideas in the other.

Maybe it was the alcohol they were sipping, but the two musical loners decided to try to collaborate.

The day after the party, both Dustin and Heidi regretted their commitment. But, being professionals, neither one wanted to back out. They both separately decided to just ride it out, so they could get on with their real work.

Getting together was a problem. Heidi was used to working late at night while Dustin always sat down at his piano first thing in the morning. They compromised on an afternoon session.

The day of the session they met at a studio. Everything was awkward—from who was going to sit at the piano first to which ideas they would pursue. The crackle that had filled their conversation was missing from the session.

The first session was a failure. Both Heidi and Dustin felt they had wasted valuable time and money. But neither was willing to call the entire project a failure. They agreed to meet again the next week. During the days between sessions, both songwriters worked harder than ever. They worked on pieces that they thought would complement the other's talents.

As for the second session, revelation was key. The beginning was still awkward, but as each presented their ideas for the other, they found new inspiration. At the end of the session they had not one, but three solid songs. They changed their goal from working together to produce one song to producing an entire album of material.

They stopped working out of a rented studio because they needed more time to work out the finer points of each song. They spent all day with each other creating musical magic for three weeks. At the end, the duo, as they now thought of themselves, had produced the best work of their careers.

However, they were still nervous. They felt that something was missing. They sent a demo of their album to their mutual producer acquaintance. He loved it. He quickly got them into the studio and made a few seemingly minor changes, but the result was lightening in a bottle.

They were soon the hottest act in town. Different labels were fighting over the right to sign them. They debuted one of their songs to a stunned crowd at a dive bar off Sunset Boulevard.

The recognition that they both had always wanted for their art was finally here. Their record was a hit, playing everywhere. Magazines put them on the cover, TV shows invited them for interviews and performances and they received awards.

For the first time in their lives they had fans. People were touched by their music. It had connected with a generation.

Dustin and Heidi would go on to have a long and successful career. During one interview the duo was asked what the secret to their success was. Why did they suddenly break through after so many years in the industry?

Dustin and Heidi quickly said that it was collaboration. The two of them plus their producer were able to create something together greater than the sum of the separate parts. Collaboration was like a secret superpower that allowed their music to go from proficient to profound.

For Your Consideration

Use the space below to answer the question with truth and transparency.

What is your perspective on collaborating with people and groups who do not share your culture or opinions on most things?

MEDITATE ON THIS

Write the following quotation and Scripture in a journal. Then critically think about each one and write how each one speaks to you. That is, how is each one renewing your mindset on the principle of collaborating being key to your fulfillment in life and spirituality?

Quotation

Collaborations work best this way; when there's a mutual desire to see what the other side adds. You know that what you're making on your own has value but the sum is more than the parts and every part knows it.
— Ahmir Questlove Thompson

Scripture

Two are better than one, because they have a good reward for their labor. For if they fall, one will lift up his companion. But woe to him who is alone when he falls, for he has no one to help him up.

Again, if two lie down together, they will keep warm; but how can one be warm alone? Though one may be overpowered by another, two can withstand him. And a threefold cord is not quickly broken.
Ecclesiastes 4:9-12

Self-Assessment

Answer each question fully and to the best of your ability. Remember, because there are no judgments or wrong answers in whatever you write, strive to be transparent.

1. How can collaboration multiply your time and efforts?

   _____

   _____

   _____

   _____

2. What type of mindset is needed to collaborate?

   _____

   _____

   _____

   _____

3. Recall your first collaborative effort. What did it feel like? What would you do differently after reading how collaboration is done?

   _____

   _____

   _____

   _____

TAKE ACTION

1. I will change these behaviors to become a better collaborator by

    _____

    _____

    _____

    _____

2. These attributes of collaboration are most important because

    _____

    _____

    _____

    _____

RELENTLESS

The definition to me is being headstrong, hard, constant, endless and non-stop. I feel that when you are these things while remaining goal-oriented, nothing is impossible. I've learned so much unlearning habits I was exposed to as a youngster. For instance, when things got hard and adversity hit, many would say 'Tuff luck; bad break; it just wasn't meant to be...' I steer free from that energy and those generations of caped behavior and try to raise the bar and change the narrative. Seeing is believing!

Caron Butler

RE·LENT·LESS

demanding more of yourself than anyone else could ever demand of you, knowing that every time you stop, you still do more. You must do more. The minute your mind thinks, "Done," your instincts say, "Next."

7

Tiger Woods. Winning for this golfer is not the objective. Excellence is. Woods knows that if he relentlessly pursues this one thing, the win will follow. Which is why after his so-called fall from grace a few years ago, he continued his chase for improbable wins. After a five-year slump in the ratings as all-time best golfer, Woods's relentlessness in excellence paid off in September 2018 with a major victory at the PGA Tour where he was crowned champion[2].

Before his latest triumph, many of his fair-weather fans had grown weary of him with all the losses. They erroneously assumed his career had reached its end, that Woods had peaked years before, and had nothing left to give. However, many more believed he still had more wins in his talented hands and would once again find his rhythm and make a comeback as all-time best golfer. Like everyone else for the previous 1,900 days, they witnessed him time and again enter major championship games only to finish well outside of the top 10 position. Nevertheless, they were relentless in their support of him, and Woods never gave up either despite the nagging back pain, insomnia and countless stories of personal issues that pursued him. Being out of the game's top leaders became more of an incentive to keep at his game until the excellence returned and once again the aging golfer would return to the winners' circle. In September of 2018, Woods proved relentlessness pays off. Today, given all that he inexorably overcame to win the PGA Tour, all of us—despite our various, personal opinions of him or his game—are

---

[2] https://www.pga.com/news/pga-tour/tiger-woods-comeback-history

compelled to call Tiger Woods champion once again.

Do You Live a 'Relentless' Life?

On a scale of one to five (with five being 'most passionate', how passionate are you about pursuing fulfillment? How dedicated are you to ensuring wholeness is a theme of your life-style? Truth is, relentlessness should be the compelling force behind just about everything you do to lead a fulfilled life. Otherwise, contentment may always elude you. The reason for this is that contentment, though it's a constitutional right, must be *pursued*. Inherent in a pursuit to anything is relentlessness.

Success rarely just happens. There are no shortcuts or elevators to it. It is chased after, hunted down, if you will, with a seriousness to stick to the hunt until the goal is reached and the mission is accomplished. Let's face it: being able to check off goals and pursue a vision until it is achieved leaves a magnanimous feeling of success that's almost second to none.

Relentlessness is a state of mind. With it comes a mental determination to be accountable, to show up when you said you were going to, to push yourself *every* day, to challenge yourself to do better the next should you make a misstep this time, to make a commitment to setting goals and achieving them, to carry on regardless of your circumstances, to face down your fears and soldier on. In a word, relentlessness is the constant condition of your mindset. Unless it's your daily disposition, whatever you want to do or accomplish in life will seem unnecessarily arduous and near impossible.

By no means are we unrealistic authors. We realize life throws us unexpected curve balls, and we have not been exempted from them in our personal lives. That is why we try to live a life of intentional relentlessness.

One cautionary note before we close this discussion on the word relentless. Do not confuse relentless with ruthless. These two words could not be any more different than up and down. Relentless refers to a person who will not give up and who will persist. Ruthless means a person who gets what they want without regard to mercy. A ruthless person, therefore, is rough and does not care about others. And when it comes to success, research suggests that being ruthless will more than likely not help you be successful. As it turns out, ruthless people leave behind a trail of burned bridges and sometimes end up in suffering terrible consequences. Contrarily, relentless people have a goal to never stop getting better at what they do and to change as many lives as they can along the way. Pass this on: relentless people care about things and people beyond themselves.

A Story about Being Relentless

During a first-grade parent-teacher conference, Ms. Giles, a middle-aged teacher, told young Sharon's parents that their daughter would never learn to read. She told them that she understood the law required them to have Sharon in school, but that it was a waste of time to teach her.

Elizabeth quivered with rage. She vowed that not only would Sharon learn to read, but that her daughter would go on to be far more educated and discerning than Ms. Giles. Elizabeth set aside two hours every day to work with Sharon on her reading. She broke up the work into four 30-minute sessions. After the first few days, Elizabeth realized that there was something not right with Sharon's eyes.

The eye doctor told Elizabeth that not only did Sharon need glasses, but he also told her that Elizabeth was dyslexic and that her eye muscles were underdeveloped. The doctor suggested some exercises that they could do at home to strengthen the eye muscles, some literature about dyslexia, and a prescription for eyeglasses.

On the way home from the eye doctor, Elizabeth stopped by Walmart and picked up everything that she would need to setup a physical therapy space at home to help Sharon build strength in her eye muscles. That night Elizabeth didn't sleep. Instead, she learned everything she could about dyslexia.

Once Sharon began wearing her glasses, her grades immediately improved, but she continued to struggle reading basic words. Ms. Giles told Elizabeth that she didn't think Sharon's problem was dyslexia. She felt that the real problems were lack of motivation and some developmental disability.

Elizabeth provided a note from the eye doctor and went up the chain of command to ensure that her daughter would get the kind of help that she needed. Elizabeth thought Ms. Giles's words were code for Sharon being lazy and stupid.

Every night Elizabeth and Sharon completed exercises that would strengthen Sharon's eye muscles. During the exercises, Elizabeth would play audiobooks of different stories for Sharon. Sharon began to love hearing the stories.

After the exercises, Elizabeth and Sharon would work on various reading strategies to help Sharon adjust to her dyslexia. However, most nights, Sharon would cry that she didn't want to learn to read. She would sob about how much she hated school and how she was sure that she would never pass the first grade. During those times, Elizabeth never scolded Sharon for these outbursts. Instead, she offered as much encouragement as she could.

Spring break came around and Sharon brought home some samples of her work from school. Elizabeth was going through them when she noticed that Sharon's handwriting had greatly improved over the past several months. The two of them hadn't even done any work on her handwriting. But Elizabeth took this as a sign that all the work was starting to pay off.

During the brief break from school, Elizabeth and Sharon refused to ease off the daily routine of eye and reading exercises. Sharon cried less frequently now, but Elizabeth wondered if her daughter harbored a quiet resentment of books and anything that seemed like schoolwork.

Sharon had a follow-up appointment with the eye doctor. He was surprised by how much strength Sharon's eye muscles had gained. He said that it was the fastest improvement that he had ever seen! When she heard the wonderful news, Sharon gave her mom a rare smile.

Towards the end of the school year, Sharon took a series of standardized tests. To ease her anxiety, Elizabeth told her daughter that she didn't care how well she did on the tests. She just wanted her to try her best.

Sharon refused to discuss the tests with her mother. All she would say was that they were fine.

With the improvement in the strength of Sharon's eye muscles, Elizabeth had eased off the eye exercises and replaced them with additional reading drills and practices. Each one was focused on teaching Sharon to deal with her dyslexia instead of trying to fight it or ignore it. The tears quickly returned.

The week before school ended for the year, a big envelope from the district arrived in the mail. Elizabeth thought that it might have to do with all the trouble she was causing in trying to get the school to make some accommodation for Sharon's dyslexia. Instead, it was the standardized test results. Elizabeth sighed, bracing herself for the worst and opened the envelope. As she read through the results, her eyes filled with tears. She set down the results and began to weep into her hands. Hearing her mom's cries, Sharon came into the room to see what the problem was. Alongside her crying mother, Sharon saw the test results down on the couch. Sharon began to cry too.

"Mom, I swear I did my best. I swear. I'm so sorry," She cried.

Elizabeth smiled. She ran over and hugged Sharon.

"I know you did. I want you to see what the test results are," Elizabeth whispered.

Sharon hesitated, but she relented and let her mother read through the results. As she heard her mother quote the results, she began to shake her head in disbelief and confusion. Sharon heard how she was above grade level in every area. Her reading level had been assessed as being at First Semester Third Grade.

"You did it, Sharon!" Elizabeth exclaimed. Sharon smiled and shook her head.

"No, Mom, you did it. You didn't give up on me. You

wouldn't let me quit."

The two hugged.

Sharon decided to use a special word her mom had taught her recently as she expressed her relief at test scores. "Mom, you were relentless. Thank you."

The next morning Elizabeth made a copy of the test results and highlighted the reading results. She went into Sharon's class before school and placed the results on Ms. Giles's desk.

For Your Consideration

Use the space below to answer the following questions with openness and transparency.

1. Have you been relentless in spreading the Good News?

2. What do you think Ms. Giles's response would be?

MEDITATE ON THIS

Write the following quotation and Scriptures in a journal. Then critically think about each one and write how it speaks to you. That is, how is each one renewing your mindset about your fulfillment in living and your spirituality?

Quotation

Gratitude was never meant to be an excuse for giving up on the obstacles God has put before you. Some of the most magical things he can bring us require faith and a lot of planning.
— Shannon L. Alder

Scriptures

Therefore let us pursue the things which make for peace and the things by which one may edify another.
Romans 14:19

Do you not know that in a race all the runners run, but only one gets the prize? Run in such a way as to get the prize. Everyone who competes in the games goes into strict training. They do it to get a crown that will not last, but we do it to get a crown that will last forever. Therefore I do not run like someone running aimlessly; I do not fight like a boxer beating the air. No, I strike a blow to my body and make it my slave so that after I have preached to others, I myself will not be disqualified for the prize.
I Corinthians 9:24-27

SELF-ASSESSMENT

Answer each question fully and to the best of your ability. Remember, because there are no judgments or wrong answers in whatever you write, strive to be transparent.

1. What do you think are positive and negative aspects of being relentless?

   _____

   _____

   _____

   _____

2. How can your own behavior move from relentlessness to ruthlessness?

   _____

   _____

   _____

   _____

3. What "burned bridges" have you created that you now regret?

   _____

   _____

   _____

   _____

4. How is being relentless associated with success and a sense of fulfillment and spirituality?

   _____

   _____

   _____

   _____

TAKE ACTION

1. I will be more

    _____

    _____

    _____

    _____

    to be relentless, but not ruthless. I will

    _____

    _____

    _____

    _____

2. To achieve the following, I will be intentionally relentless.

    _____

    _____

    _____

    _____

TRUST

Gives you the permission to give people direction, get everyone aligned and give them the energy to get the job done. Trust enables you to execute with excellence and produce extraordinary results.

Douglas R. Conant

TRUST

firm belief in the reliability, truth, ability, or strength of someone or something

8

O nce upon a time, there was an eight-year old little girl who was happily jumping rope on a train. She seemed totally oblivious to the thunderstorm that was raging on the outside. Pelts of rain pounded the fast-moving locomotive while the gleeful little girl continued showing off her skills in jumping rope without missing a beat. All the passengers simply stared at her in disbelief. On the one hand, they admired her courage to play happily while rain pelted the train and the sound of thunder roared on louder and louder. On the other hand, they wondered how she could jump rope with such cheer. Finally, one of the passengers could stand it no longer and spoke what was invariably on everybody else's mind. "Little girl, how can you jump rope so happily? Don't you know there is a terrible thunderstorm outside? Aren't you scared something bad is going to happen?"

The little girl, unbothered by his question, continued skipping rope and responded in a matter-of-fact tone, "No, because my daddy is the engineer."

Unlike her fellow passengers, the little girl extended something to the engineer that the others just couldn't bring themselves to give him. The engineer had her trust. The little girl didn't hope that they would all be brought to safety. She knew they would be because she trusted her father would do all he could to make that happen. The storm raged, and still she trusted him to deliver her and the rest of the passengers to safety. And because she trusted him, she never doubted his ability to engineer that train well, despite the adverse weather conditions.

Trust is so essential in building and maintaining relationships (relational, familial, business, and otherwise that we decided to make it one of the words to pass on to you— albeit with an observation from our experiences in working with people. Those who try to do life without ever trusting another person tend to short-change themselves of a fulfilled life. They refuse to trust because it opens them up to being vulnerable. And no one wants the uncertainty that comes with being vulnerable. Yet trust may be the single most fundamental source to thriving relationships. Compared to the importance to love, trust still comes out on top, namely because without it, there is no unconditional love between two people. We guess you could say trust undergirds love.

Our hope is that this brief discussion affirms the importance of trust and its necessity to your journey to fulfillment and spirituality.

Trusting You Get It

Admittedly trust is a choice. To be trustworthy is a choice and to trust another is a choice. Our position is that unless we all choose to extend this grace to others, then think what life would be like without it? Take marriage, for example. It is a covenant between two people that must be predicated upon trust. You thought it was love, didn't you? No, it's trust. Love matters, but it's one of those emotions that we feel today, but may not feel tomorrow, for various reasons. In situations like this, it is then that we must *choose to trust* our loved one if and when the love is swinging from one point of the pendulum to the other.

There is no other word we can pass on that conveys integrity as much as trust. If someone trusts you, it means that they have confidence in your integrity and that you will act with honor. No wonder trust is integral in our personal relationships and the business world. It could be the most valued quality in a person that employers desire in their employees and individuals in their partners. Being trustworthy puts you on the moral high ground every time and indubitably signals to people that you can be trusted with more and more responsibilities. Do not be surprised by the positive reactions to you.

Cracked Mirror

How well do you trust a cracked mirror? Most likely, not much. For obvious reasons, a cracked mirror can significantly distort the image. Well, trust can sometimes be like a mirror. If left intact, everything in the relationship is fine. However, if the trust is ever breached (cracked), then repair to it would be difficult. And, if there is an attempt to repair it, the process may call for hours of healing, maybe even outside help, like counseling, to assist in mending things back together. This scenario rings true regardless of the type of relationship where trust is broken, be it a marriage, business, friendships, and so on. Where there is any incident where the trust was ruptured, then the relationship has been put at risk. An unfortunate consequence is that the relationship may never be repaired.

We said earlier that trust is a choice—whether you pass it on or someone has passed it on to you. In either case, remember that trust, as necessary as it is in relationships, is a delicate quality. When guarded, it has the most incredible feeling; if risked or harmed in any way, it could lead to irreparable damage to the relationship—almost impossible to repair, just like a cracked mirror.

A Story about Trust

Joao was tall and dangerously thin. His boyish face and frail-looking body led many tourists to mistake him for being 15. But the hard look in Joao's eyes betrayed the hard life of a man 21 years older. Joao thought he was 20, but that was only based on the information his gang leader had given him when he was old enough to start asking questions.

He was raised on the streets of El Salvador. He was told that his parents had abandoned him. Later he discovered while hiding during a drunken brawl between two of the gang members who raised him that the same gang had killed his parents during a botched robbery of their fish market stall. They kept Joao alive because they thought he would make a good beggar.

Joao left the slums that night but stayed nearby because he had nowhere to go. To this point in his life, he had been a beggar, a thief, a lookout and a magnet for abuse. Joao knew he loved the sea. He was deceptively strong. He tried to get work as a fisherman, but the tight knit community was wary of a stranger with no past. A few men thought they recognized Joao as one of the boys who frequently stole from the various market stalls and warehouses near the waterfront. They were not wrong.

Determined not to steal any longer than he had to, Joao would spy on the fishermen. He watched them ready their nets early in the morning. He watched them launch their boats and waited for their return.

Out of desperation to learn all their secrets, Joao stowed away on one of the fishing boats. He was discovered out at sea as the men were headed to the fishing grounds. Not believing his story, the captain ordered Joao tossed overboard. "The world would be better without you," the captain said.

Joao hit the water and flailed around. Even though he had lived his entire life within walking distance from the ocean, he did not know how to swim. He swallowed seawater and began to sink below the waves when a pair of huge, weathered hands pulled him up and threw him in a boat. The captain said, "I could come get you if I would be responsible for you. Can I trust you? Because if not, I will throw you back."

Joao was still coughing. He nodded "yes" vigorously and managed to get out the words, "You can trust me."

"We'll see. My name is Lucas." After that, the rescuer said nothing else as he sailed Joao to shore.

Lucas gave Joao some food and let him sleep under his family's truck on a piece of cardboard. Lucas told Joao he would teach Joao to be a fisherman and would make sure that he got paid, but Joao would have to pay him back for the food and the sleeping arrangements.

Joao readily agreed. He did not want to be a thief, but he had no plans to stay with Lucas. If he had learned one thing on the streets of El Salvador it was that trust was a prelude to a painful death.

The other fishermen told Lucas he was crazy to trust the strange boy. Lucas never replied to their taunts and accusations.

Joao was a fast learner. He quickly mastered the basic tasks he was given, careful to always do more than what was expected. Joao was shocked when Lucas first paid him. Joao didn't believe he would really get any money from Lucas.

Months passed, and Joao's body filled out. The regular diet and strenuous work agreed with him. He now looked like a fisherman. He gained additional scars and calloused hands. Slowly, others in the crew gave him a grudging respect. Joao never asked for more than his share. He never gave any of his excess. He refused to tell Lucas or anyone what he did with his money. Lucas had told him that his debt would be paid off in two weeks and then he was free to continue making a full wage.

Joao decided it was time to leave and strike out on his own now that he had the basic skills. It was better to leave than be betrayed by Lucas.

On what was going to be Joao's last trip with the crew, a driving rain and powerful wind pounded their vessel. The captain had gone down near the bow to yell at a careless crewman when the ship lurched and sent the captain overboard. Joao watched the man who had tried to kill him months before fall into the sea. He looked around, but nobody else had seen the captain go over yet.

Joao turned his back to the bow. He began to yell that the captain had gone over. Members of the crew came scrambling over to toss the captain a rope. Lucas was giving orders and took control of the rope. Joao saw one of the floats they sometimes used on their nets sitting loose on the deck. He grabbed it, ran to the bow, and jumped into the fomenting waves. He held tightly onto the flat and searched for the captain. The captain was trying in vain to grab at the rope, but the waves were too strong and kept pulling the rope away from him. Joao, who had learned to swim since his last plunge into the ocean, but was still awkward in the water, maneuvered over to the rope. He tied it to the float and swam to the captain and grabbed him under his armpit and pulled him along. The men on the boat saw what Joao was doing and pulled him and the captain up, both of whom were clutching to the float for dear life.

Once aboard, the crew headed back to shore and the captain and Joao were taken to get dry. Nobody said anything to the captain or Joao until the boat was safely docked. Lucas and Joao walked back home in silence for the first few minutes.

"Why did you save the life of the man who had tried to kill you?" Lucas asked. "Nobody would have known had you not gone for help. He would have drowned without you risking everything and jumping in."

Joao stopped walking and looked at Lucas. "I learned on the streets that if you trust someone, they would take advantage of you. Nobody in my gang ever trusted me. But, you who had no reason to save me, trusted me. I did not owe the captain anything, but I owed you. I wanted you to know I would not betray your trust."

Lucas smiled. "Joao, I trust you. Do you trust me?"

"You have pulled me from the sea twice, even though it would have been easier for you to let me die. I trust you."

Lucas laughed and said, "Tonight, you will sleep inside my house and not under our truck. Tomorrow you and I will find a boat and start our fishing business. We will be partners." Lucas stretched out his hand towards Joao. Joao stared at the man with wonder. He kept waiting for Lucas to pull his hand back or to laugh at the joke of trust. But, he just stood there with his hand extended towards Joao. He kept it there far longer than was comfortable. Finally, Joao reached his hand out and the men clasped hands, sealing their new partnership with mutual trust.

For Your Consideration

Use the space below to answer the following question. Remember, there's no judgment on your answer, so be as transparent as possible.

Do you trust someone for whom you care, yet do not have trust *in* them? Explain.

MEDITATE ON THIS

Write the following quotation and Scripture in a journal. Then critically think about each one and write how it speaks to you. That is, how is each one renewing your mindset about your fulfillment in living and your spirituality?

Quotation

Trust but verify. – Ronald Reagan

Scripture

And those who know Your name will put their trust in You; For You, Lord, have not forsaken those who seek You.
Psalm 9:10

Self-Assessment

Answer each question fully and to the best of your ability. Remember, because there are no judgments or wrong answers in whatever you write, strive to be transparent.

1. What is your own definition of trust?

    _____

    _____

    _____

    _____

2. What causes you to lose trust in someone?

    _____

    _____

    _____

    _____

TAKE ACTION

1. I will show others that I am trustworthy by

   _____

   _____

   _____

   _____

2. When I lose trust in someone, I will

   _____

   _____

   _____

   _____

INSPIRE

People will forget what you said, people will forget what you did, but people will never forget how you made them feel.

Carl W. Buehner with addition by

Maya Angelou

In·Spire

*to encourage someone by making them feel
confident and eager to do something*

9

In 1986, much of our nation, including young children, watched in disbelief as Space Shuttle Challenger quickly exploded into pieces within 73 seconds of blasting off from Cape Canaveral, Florida. Onboard the disastrous flight were seven of America's extraordinary astronauts. Among the seven was breakthrough educator and lasting inspiration, Sharon Christa McAuliffe, affectionately known as Christa.

Though she was not the first woman or American woman in space, Christa McAuliffe became America's first classroom teacher to experience life as an astronaut, even though it was a brief life. What makes the Bostonian so inspirational is not that she died young and tragically, but that she died proving that educators have so much to offer in space exploration. Specifically, Christa's presence among the seven inspired education reformers to take a closer look at what happens in the classroom where girls are considered, especially when it comes to science and math education. In case you are not aware, there was a time when females were not encouraged as much they are now to seek opportunities in science where they could join their male counterparts as researchers working on the cures to fatal diseases. Unfortunately, their aversion to anything science-related or math-related may have begun in the very place Christa knew could make an extraordinary difference to a child's life—the classroom. In fact, Christa's intention that fatal day was to lead a class from space. At any rate, it was once the classroom that education research shows that girls in science and math classes were called upon less than boys. What this eventually translates into is fewer females dominating in the sciences where they could become doctors, scientists, researchers, and so on, just like their male counterparts.

Space exploration is where the 37-year-old social studies teacher wanted to inspire her students and the rest of us. And so she did. Her inclusion in space exploration and subsequent tragic end helped bring vital attention to what was happening to the education of females. Inspired in part by Christa's participation in the Teaches in Space Project, education reform began calling for classroom teachers to push the envelope where girls are concerned in what is known as STEM (Science, Technology, Engineering, Math) classes. That is, ask girls the tough questions once reserved for boys! They can handle them with as much as ease as anyone. Although she was a social studies teacher, Christa proved that progression in science should not be gender-based, and we believe, had she lived, she would have spoken up more and more about inclusiveness of females in science.

Today, there are 40 schools worldwide named after America's first teacher in space. Her work has also inspired her alma mater, Framingham State College, to establish a building and program in her name. The McAuliffe Center works to change ways children approach science. For example, they strive to eliminate timidity and replace it with a love of exploration and creativity. To do this, the Center replicated Houston's Mission Control where visiting students can solve problems that may arise in space flight. Her alma mater has not been the only entity inspired by Christa's moment in science. In 2004, she was posthumously awarded the *Congressional Space Medal of Honor*. And, since her death, schools and various honors across the nation have been named in her memory. There have also been grants named after Christa for teachers who inspire students to achieve well. Christa's memory has been honored by film as she was portrayed by Karen Allen in a movie. She even inspired an original song by Carly Simon in 2006.

Before you convince yourself that you could not possibly be

as inspiring as Christa—don't. The beautiful thing about inspiring others is that it does not take a special or an unusual talent, gifting or skills. What it takes is a willingness to put yourself out there to make a difference to the lives of others, just like Christa did.

Inspiring People, Changing Lives

Is there anyone in your life—past or present—who tends to be enthusiastic most of the time? Are they positive thinkers? And do they seem to look for ways to encourage others most of the time? Chances are that person spends a good deal of their own life inspiring the lives of others, and in the course of doing so, they change lives. That's just how powerful inspiration is. With just the right encouragement and support, inspiration can change the course of another person's life. Pause for a second here and think about your own life, specifically focus on how you wound up where you are right now. Who inspired your steps? What words did they pass on to you that propelled you from one level to the next? Then think about how you can do the same for someone else. The beauty of it is that you do not have to work to change hundreds of lives. Only one will do. Many good things have come out of one. For instance, from one couple, many nations and ethnicities were born. Some recent school shootings were either stopped or prevented by the actions of one person, not a squadron of police officers.

For Your Consideration

We wanted to conclude this chapter differently than we did the others. It comes from an inspiration from Craig Robinson, Vice-President of Player Development for the New York Knicks. Craig believes inspiring people to reach their goals is a valuable service and strives to inspire others regularly. With that in mind, rather than merely concluding with a question for your consideration, we wanted you to pause a bit and meditate on a few more thoughts about the word inspire and its myriad of meanings.

For starters, inspire is synonymous to teaching, encouraging, mentoring, helping, motivating, and influencing. Keeping each of these similar meanings in mind, what person(s) come to mind? What words did they pass along to you that supported your dreams to be whatever you are right now?

According to one of our colleagues, an underutilized aspect of inspiring others is empathizing with them. Do you agree with this thought?

Finally, in terms of your own capacity to lead well, how often do you think about looking *to be inspired* by those you try to inspire as a way to grow your leadership development?

A Story about Inspiring Others

Ken stood in the back of the gallery watching the throngs of art collectors, art lovers, and art critics circulate through his latest ceramics exhibition. A stern, middle-aged woman spotted Ken and strode across the floor, looking much like a lion springing on a hapless gazelle, Ken thought.

She was an art reporter for a big national magazine. Ken had read her work for years and admired the way she molded words, much like the way he attempted to mold clay. Both tried to make something beautiful and profound out of something ordinary and profane.

The reporter introduced herself and quickly launched into an interrogation. She wanted to know about Ken's background, his studio, and how he had burst onto the scene causing a sensation with his exhibition. Ken gave the same practiced answers he had given the other journalists and interviewers over the past week.

Then the reporter asked, "What inspires your work?"

Ken paused and thought back on the past five years. He had received a Master's in Fine Arts. He loved working with ceramics, but he also loved to eat, so he set out to find a job that paid him enough to work at his potter's wheel and pay his bills. He ended up working a variety of short-term adjunct professor gigs at small colleges across the Midwest. The work was great. He loved teaching his craft. The pay was tolerable, but Ken rarely had time to just create.

It took only a year for Ken to realize that teaching wasn't his passion. He spent the next two and half years scrimping and saving as much as he could as he frequently changed schools. He worked odd jobs, and he mostly avoided working on his own ceramics. When he finally had enough money, he quit teaching and went out into the world to find the inspiration for his next work.

Ken traveled to Asia, Europe, South America, and Africa. He spent time viewing ancient ruins, touring museums and inspecting the finest potteries the world had ever known. He watched the sun set on four different continents. He wrote pages and pages of notes and took thousands of pictures. But, after traveling around the world, he still had no idea what his life's work should be. Unfortunately, Ken had not found one shred of inspiration in his travels.

Despondent, Ken sat a bar in the tropical paradise of Phuket, Thailand, with his head in his hands while waiting for his iced tea to come. He had just spent his last American dollar and was having to face the fact that he had to go home, after having wasted six months of his life. A small man with white hair and a white beard sat down on a bar stool next to Ken. He looked like a garden gnome that had come to life, dressed in shorts and sandals.

"Hard day?" the man asked Ken.

Ken looked up, and for reasons he never understood, told his whole sad story to the stranger.

"How much pottery have you made this past six months?" the man asked.

"None. I've been trying to find some inspiration. I need to be inspired to create art," Ken said.

"I thought you said you were a ceramics artist."

"I am," Ken said, rolling his eyes upward, frustrated that the stranger didn't appear to understand the depth of his problems.

"If you aren't creating art, how can you be an artist? A writer writes. A painter paints. A fisherman fishes. If you aren't doing the work, how do you know whether or not you have been inspired?"

Dumbfounded, Ken stared at the little man. The man hopped off the stool and walked out of the bar. Ken drank his ice tea and hurried to pack his things.

Within a week, Ken was back home. The first thing he did was buy some supplies and started to work at his wheel. His first pieces were awful. His hands had forgotten how to hold and mold the clay at the same time. The first few batches Ken smashed with a hammer. He couldn't stand to look at them. He had no idea what he wanted, but these were not it. He figured that he had enough money left to survive for three months before he would absolutely need cash.

He worked 16-hour days creating junk, but after two weeks he noticed his creations were improving. His body was remembering what it took to create decent art. After six weeks, he pulled out his most recent batch from the kiln. He had hoped to find some treasures, but it was just more junk.

He began pacing, thinking about what he could do to get some more money. Mumbling to himself, Ken went over to the cooling rack and picked up a plate he had made and threw it against the wall, shattering it. He got hold of a broom and began to sweep his failure off the cement floor. He saw something in the pattern of the debris. He dropped the broom and ran to his studio and his wheel.

All through the night, Ken worked feverishly on his inspiration. For the first time since he had gotten home, being at the wheel was a joy. He was staying out of love, not discipline, or desperation. He set his creations to dry and be fired. It would be a couple of weeks before he knew the results of his midnight madness. But, his soul was filled with light. He kept working and creating an astonishing number of pieces every day.

Ken remembered crying when he saw the late nigh batch come back from the kiln. They looked exactly like he had seen them in his mind. Shortly after that, he put some pictures of his work online. His art went viral.

Ken looked at the reporter. He realized he had zoned off.

"I'm sorry. What was my inspiration?" Ken said. The reporter nodded.

"Work. Work was my inspiration," Ken said. "Isn't that kind of circular?" the reporter asked.

"No. You see fisherman fish and artists create art. I just kept creating until I made something good. The inspiration didn't come from outside of me, it came from inside of me. If you want to be inspired, you have to show up and do the work. All I wanted to do was to create ceramics that inspire others to make beautiful things. To do that, I had to spend the time working."

Unsatisfied with Ken's explanation, the reporter sauntered outside.

Ken smiled and thought about the strange little man that he met half a world away. He taught Ken that inspiration only comes after putting in the work.

For Your Consideration

Use the space available to answer the questions with truth and transparency.

What do you think it takes to help some people understand that money may not be the inspiration some think that it is?

If you were awarded a prestigious prize such as the Nobel prize for doing something inspirational, what would it be?

MEDITATE ON THIS

Write the following quotation and Scripture in a journal. Then critically think about each one and write how each speaks to you. That is, how is each one renewing your mindset on the principle of inspiration being key to your fulfillment in life and your spirituality?

Quotation

Every scar that you have is a reminder not just that you got hurt, but that you survived.

- Michelle Obama

Scripture

For God has not given us a spirit of fear, but of power and of love and of a sound mind.

2 Timothy 1:7

SELF-ASSESSMENT

Answer each question fully and to the best of your ability. Remember, because there are no judgments or wrong answers in whatever you write, strive to be transparent.

1. In what way(s) are you inspired to achieve your goals?

    _____

    _____

    _____

    _____

2. Who have you inspired to action? What were they inspired to do?

    _____

    _____

    _____

    _____

3. Where do you get your inspiration?

    _____

    _____

    _____

    _____

TAKE ACTION

1. I will foster inspiration in others by

   _____

   _____

   _____

   _____

2. I will stay inspired to take action by

   _____

   _____

   _____

   _____

PEACE

True peace is not merely the absence of tension; it is the presence of justice.

Dr. Martin Luther King, Jr.

PEACE

a mental or spiritual condition marked by a lack of conflict and freedom from fear of violence

10

Thirty-eight packs a day. That's how many cigarettes she smoked just to cope with everyday situations. Supermodel Gisele Bundchen recently shared that, before she finally found a sense of peace, crushing panic attacks controlled her life. There was a time she couldn't do simple things like use an elevator or travel through tunnels to get from place to place without experiencing a panic attack. She tried dealing with the attacks as best she could. Smoking a pack of cigarettes a day was her answer, but it was far from being a cure. Over time, the panic attacks became worse and worse, prompting the beautiful 5'11" supermodel to seriously contemplate committing suicide to end them. Fortunately, more than anything else, she wanted to live. For that reason, Bundchen had finally come to a point where she decided enough was enough; she wasn't going to battle any more panic attacks. Consequently she reached outside herself for help. Along with other assistance, she changed her diet and began to experience the peace that had dodged her at one time.

Bundchen's unfortunate health issue raised an interesting observation for this book: many people lack peace for one reason or another. Like Bundchen, they pull out their own repertoire of cures for that elusive gateway to peace. When nothing seems to work, they begin pasting on smiles and doing other things to give the illusion of peace. However, behind the phony smiles and the hollow laughter remains a real, deep sadness. If you're one of those persons, we assure you there is hope. We believe that, in time and under the right circumstances, you will be able to pass on peace to another.

Catching up with Peace for a Fulfilled You

As we all know, there is a plethora of material out there on attaining peace. Many authorities have written something on the subject. It is certainly not our intention to try to re-invent the wheel on peace-attainment. However, out of our experiences, we will share a few pointers on doable, easy-to-implement strategies on attaining peace that we have shared with our constituents.

Let's begin with the mind, since nearly every emotion begins there, including peace. This means peace is not necessarily controlled by external events, which are out of our control anyway. It is an emotion from within and therefore controlled by the mind, which is home to every emotion. That's because the limbic system in the brain executes emotions, which, in non-scientific terms, means *the mind has the power to keep emotions in check*. And, who governs the mind? You do. So, what does that have to do with your peace? It means you have the emotional intelligence (the ability to identify emotions, apply them, and manage them) to *train* your brain to respond to something with peace, instead of reactionary emotions like anger. Start with training the brain to pause and think about what was said or done. This pause gives us long enough for the brain time to process without a lot of emotion involved. Then identify the best, well-constructed response to apply to something negative you heard against you or to something negative that happened to you.

Here is something else that brings peace. Taking responsibility for your actions and reactions. Younger generations call this "my bad". Believe it or not, your peace can be influenced greatly on your humility (another word to pass on). For example, ask forgiveness when you're the one who offended another. Training your ego and mindset will assist you greatly in obtaining peace.

During challenges for your peace, we also suggest being cognizant of what you watch, listen to and read. Avoid media that evoke anger, bitterness, sadness and other reactionary emotions, until you have fully mastered controlling your thoughts, which, in turn, control your emotions. Instead, try meditating on materials that teach you how to control your emotions. Otherwise, you inadvertently risk having your peace taken hostage by negative emotions, leaving you to focus on being intentional about ways to release it and maintain it.

For Your Consideration

Use the space below to answer the following question with openness and transparency.

Why is it easier to take responsibility for offending, say, a non-loved one, than it is a loved one?

A STORY ABOUT PEACE

Shayla leaned her head against the window on the passenger side while glaring at the city as her mother drove. Her hands were in her lap, balled up into tight fists, ready to punish anyone who dared get close.

"I'm sorry about this, honey. But I have to go to this training or I lose my job," her mother said.

The car pulled to a stop behind a silver Honda with a big blond patch on the driver's side and a garbage bag that had been taped over where the back window had once been. The driver's hand lazily hung out the side of his window, flicking cigarette butts into the pothole below his hand. It was the only car Shayla had seen in worse shape than theirs in a long time.

"You could have left me home for three days. I'm not a baby. I'm 14. I can take care of myself," Shayla said, with her hands clenched even tighter as she licked her lips and stared at the man's cigarette from between her fingers. Out of the corner of her eye, Shayla saw her mother look over at her. She couldn't decide if her mother was going to smile or cry.

"I know. I trust you. You've had to spend too much time taking care of yourself as it is. I just don't trust the rest of the neighborhood. If something happened to you—I just don't know what I'd do. You're all—." Her mother began to tear up.

The light changed, and the car began moving again. Her mother willed the tears to stop.

Shayla relaxed her grip. The cigarette attached to the man's arm disappeared back into his car.

"What's so bad about Mama Ella?" Her mother asked.

"Nothing."

The truth was Shayla hated going to her grandma's because the woman was always happy. Nothing ever seemed to upset her, which just seemed off to Shayla somehow. She also hated how Mama Ella always wanted to tell her about her dad. It tore Shayla up inside every time she heard his name or saw his picture. Why didn't anyone understand that?

The car pulled into the broken driveway of Mama Ella's house a short while later. It really wasn't that far away, if you could drive.

Mama Ella had been sitting on her front porch, fanning herself and drinking a glass of iced tea. She stood up and hobbled down the stairs as Shayla and her mom pulled up.

"Gracious, child, you look more like your daddy every time I see you. But, you've got your momma's eyes." Mama Ella embraced Shayla in a tight bear hug. Shayla clenched her fists again.

"Thank you so much for watching Shayla, Mama Ella."

Mama Ella released Shayla to speak to her mother. "Watch her? Why Shayla watches herself. She's such a good girl, and never gives me a bit of trouble. You just go on to your training. I should thank you for letting me spend time with Shayla."

Shayla felt guilty hearing Mama Ella lie about how easy she was to get along with. She felt even worse when she looked at her mother's face and realized her mother knew it was lie.

Mama Ella insisted on carrying something for Shayla, so she gave her a pillow. Shayla always brought her own pillow because Mama Ella's pillows all smelled.

The inside of the house was even hotter than the outside. Shayla understood why Mama Ella had been enjoying the shade of the porch.

"Shayla, you go ahead and get yourself settled in the back room. I'll be out on the porch. My old bones can't handle being in this heat box."

Shayla, still feeling guilty, spoke the obligatory, "Yes, ma'am."

Shayla threw her stuff down on the bed and unleashed her clenched fists in a fury of blows on the old mattress. She tasted a few tears, and immediately stopped her assault. She willed herself to stop crying. If her mom could stop her tears, Shayla could do the same.

Unable to stand the house any longer, as the heat had made the strange smell even worse, she went out to the porch and plopped down in a chair next to her grandma.

"What's troubling you today? You seem to have a powerful anger, Miss Shayla. I'm surprised that old mattress could take that kind of thing."

Shayla clenched her fists again. Being spied on? Maybe she would just get her stuff and walk back home. She could make it by dark if she left now.

"It's okay honey. I didn't mean to invade your privacy. I may be old, but my old ears know all the sounds of this house. You know how often I heard your daddy punch that old mattress? What's so wrong that you could get so angry?"

Shayla looked up at her grandma. The woman sat there, calm like always. Her big eyes behind her big glasses made her look like an owl. Before she knew what she was doing, Shayla started yelling.

"What's wrong? What's wrong?! My daddy's dead. Shot. For doing nothing. You're his mom and you aren't even mad. You sit there every day being happy. How can you be so happy? Daddy's dead!" Shayla was shaking with pent-up rage.

"All you do is talk about him like he's still here. I can't take it. Mom doesn't trust me to be at home. I hate coming here. I hate you. I hate you! You're so old. You sit here sipping your iced tea, doing nothing, but you're still alive. It should be you that's dead, not my daddy."

Tears flowed down Shayla's cheek, she couldn't get them to stop. Just like she couldn't get her daddy's blood to stop flowing. The thought of him lying with his eyes open, bleeding out onto the pavement, made Shayla cry harder.

Mama Ella sat in silence. Shayla's eyes finally cleared enough to look at her grandma. The old woman's smile was gone, but she didn't look mad. Shayla had expected to get slapped for her words. But, Mama Ella just sat there, looking worried, but with no hint of anger.

"Child, I'm sorry that you had to carry all that around in you for all these months."

"I'm sorry, Mama Ella. I shouldn't have said those things."

"Nonsense, you deserve to feel anger and hurt. I love you no matter what you say. Plus, you're right. It should have been me. It's not right for a parent to bury their child. It's never right, even a full-grown child. The parent should die first."

Shayla looked into her grandma's eyes and blurted out, "But, why are you so happy?"

Mama Ella answered. "Happy? No. I'm not happy. I'm just at peace."

"Peace?" Shayla asked.

"Peace. I am at peace knowing your daddy lived the best life he could. I'm at peace knowing I can't change what happened. All I can do is love you like your daddy did. I feel peace."

"How can you feel peace knowing there is so much hate, knowing you can get shot for just walking outside your house?"

"Peace comes from inside Shayla. It is a choice. I choose to accept that the world is not mine to change. I choose to focus on the only thing that I can do. I can love. Loving you and your mom brings me peace. Loving the man your daddy was gives me peace."

Shayla stood up and hugged her grandma.

Three days later, Shayla's mother drove up the broken driveway. She looked tired as she got out of the car. She looked like a woman facing an unpleasant task. She stopped short when she heard the laughter. Shayla and Mama Ella were laughing on the porch. They both had glasses of iced tea and a photo album between them. It was filled with her dad's baby pictures.

Puzzled, Shayla's mom walked up the steps, "What's going on with you two?"

Shayla jumped up and hugged her mom tighter than she had in years—tighter than at the funeral even. She let go and her mom gasped.

"What's gotten into you, Miss Shayla Boynton Washington?" Shayla's mom asked with a confused smile.

"Just a little iced tea," Mama Ella said.

"I just found some peace here on the front porch with Mama Ella. Why don't you sit down and look at pictures with us for a bit?"

For Your Consideration

Use the available space below to answer each question completely and transparently.

1. What do you need peace in right now?

2. What do you do to be at peace with something you cannot control?

MEDITATE ON THIS

Write the following quotation and Scripture in a journal. Then critically think about each one and write how each one speaks to you. That is, how is each one renewing your mindset on the principle of loving being key to your fulfillment in life and spirituality?

Quotation

Peace is the result of retraining your mind to process life as it is, rather than as you think it should be.

-Dr. Wayne W. Dyer

Scripture

You will keep him in perfect peace, Whose mind is stayed on You, Because he trusts in You.

Isaiah 26:3

SELF-ASSESSMENT

*Be anxious for nothing, but in everything by prayer and
supplication, with thanksgiving, let your requests be made
known to God; and the peace of God, which surpasses all
understanding, will guard your hearts and minds through
Christ Jesus.*
Philippians 4:6-7

Answer each question fully and to the best of your ability.
Remember, because there are no judgments or wrong answers
in whatever you write, strive to be transparent.

1. What are the moments that bring peace to you?

   _____
   _____
   _____
   _____

2. Why or why are you not at peace right now?

   _____
   _____
   _____
   _____

3. Describe a time when someone had to bring you to a
   place of peace. Include ways they did so.

   _____
   _____
   _____
   _____

TAKE ACTION

1. To experience peace immediately, I will

2. For long-term sustainability of peace, I will

3. I will help others achieve peace by

FAITH

Faith is a knowledge within the heart, beyond the reach of proof.

Kahlil Gibran

FAITH

*complete confidence in someone or something;
strong belief in God or in the doctrines of a religion,
based on spiritual apprehension rather than proof*

11

For countless households across America, the holiday season can be one of the busiest times of the year. Starting around Thanksgiving or so, children begin turning in their carefully-thought-out lists of what they want for Christmas. I imagine that whatever they cannot write or spell, they draw pictures of it as best they can. And if that does not suffice, they are likely more than elated to rattle off their lists to their parents, while forgetting absolutely nothing in the recitation! No doubt their eyes light up from just picturing their parents fetching the desires of their little hearts. And, no matter how much their parents may plead to them to keep their Christmas lists at a minimum and within reason of the household budget, somehow, these children believe their parents will not turn them down. To them, Mom and Dad could make anything possible. On those grounds alone, their childlike faith in their parents is unshakeable. At an early age, children learn to apply faith with their requests. They know that, with enough hope behind their requests, something on that list will materialize. It does not matter to them how this is going to happen; all that matters is that it will happen—year after year, until they are old enough to make their own dreams come true.

I often wonder what the world would be like if more of us — especially adults—practiced the childlike faith children have growing up. It doesn't come with a lot of fancy reasoning or logic. Instead, it's refreshing, innocent and without judgment or paranoia. It's the kind of faith that does not look for a lot of answers before submitting the question. In the case of children at Christmastime, they simply hand in their lists of big-ticket items to their parents, flash an irresistible smile, and go skipping off to next thing. That's exactly how childlike faith works. You simply submit your seemingly impossible requests to the one who can best answer them, while you return to a place of rest.

Without a doubt, faith is advantageous to living a fulfilled life. With it, one can expect countless victories in seemingly impossible circumstances. Contrarily, where faith is limited, so is living a victorious life. Additionally, from a spiritual perspective, the Bible itself declares that faith is the one necessary thing needed to please the God who created everything (Hebrews 11:6). And, from its definition alone, we can see that it makes the potential possible.

Now, despite the good I know that faith brings to one's life, I want to be transparent about something. I am a realist who does not mind admitting that life is sometimes hard. It would be irresponsible of me as a pastor to not acknowledge that there are people who struggle with embracing enough faith to get them through one more day. Over the years, I have conducted numerous counseling sessions with people who, when their faith was severely challenged, gave up. From those sessions, I discovered that faith for some people is like a leaky vessel. It was once there, enabling its owner to experience fulfillment and contentment. Then, life happened in monumental terms, and faith leaked out. Despite how things appear right now, do not quit on your faith. Without it, you will be on a constant search for contentment.

Faith Is the Energy of Fulfilled Living

Faith, at its core, is exactly how Martin Luther King, Jr., once defined it. "[It] is taking the first step even when you don't see the whole staircase." In practical terms, faith is taking a seat at a beautifully prepared dinner table without thinking twice about your chair collapsing with you in it.

Think about it: you did not have to see the chair being built to place your faith in its strength and ability to hold you. Neither did you concern yourself with the manufacturer of the chair and the ability of its workers to build quality furniture. You simply took a seat believing that all would be well. Because you released your faith in that chair without worrying about its capacity to hold you, you were able to enjoy your meal and the fellowship of family and friends. It was just the energy you needed to have a great time. No stress, no drama, no angst. You can just have a good time out with loved ones.

When we take control of the mindset so that it does not rummage around in areas where it can result in stress (e.g., overthinking how a chair was made before you sit in it), then it becomes easier to put faith to work instead of an overactive imagination. This is how faith is activated. In a sense, it is you taking charge of *you.* Neither people nor circumstances determine for you what you should think about something. You are solely responsible for that. This means you can command your mind to relinquish reasoning a thing out so that your faith— your expectations that things will work out well even when it seems all odds are against you—is activated instead. A welcomed consequence is that you are in a place of peace while things begin to fall in place. It's the kind of thing that happened in the earlier example of how Christmas unfolds in many homes across America. The kids in the story were at peace because they activated faith—not anxious thoughts—in their parents, the ones who could make their impossible dreams come true. They went on in peace while their parents set about deciding what should happen. I don't know about you, but this situation reminds me of our relationship with our heavenly Father. We bring our requests to Him, leave in faith believing that He will quietly and diligently orchestrate things behind the scenes so that all things eventually work out for good.

Faith's Place in Your Spirituality

You have probably heard that we were made to thrive, not just survive. I believe that, but what does faith have to do with us thriving? From my own experiences from various roles I have fulfilled over the course of my life, I can attest that faith has unequivocally been a deciding factor in prospering at every role I was called to. This much has been clear to me: there is no way any of us can thrive in various roles we were born into or given well unless we have a relationship with God, our Creator. It is in this relationship where all things become possible. Similar to a relationship between a man and a woman, something is needed to keep the relationship functioning, lasting, and viable. For married couples, it is love. For a relationship with God, it is faith. Without it, there is no pleasing Him.

We are often presented with circumstances that seem impossible. Because we were made to thrive, we push through them. We know that if we want anything out of life, we have to be relentless about getting it. In all our getting, there is an energy we need to keep pushing, to keep hoping that there is light at the end of tunnel, though all we see for now is darkness. That energy is faith, specifically faith in God, that He is totally aware of our circumstances and has every intention of empowering us to overcome every one of them. Under pressure, faith becomes the driving force behind our prayers; it becomes the reason we level up our language from 'I can't' to 'I can do this'. In the end, every victory we experience is undergirded by faith. And like children at Christmastime, we get to come away content that the One in whom we placed our faith will take care of the desires of our hearts we placed before Him.

A Story about Faith

In some movies when someone drowns, there is a big commotion—lots of splashing and panicked cries for help. But, drowning is usually deceptively calm and quiet. It can happen in the few seconds between the time you look at your daughter in the back of the boat as she grins and marvels at the beauty of the lake, and then turn away to ask your husband a question.

That's how we lost Jenna. That's how I found my faith.

Jenna was two weeks away from her twelfth birthday. We took a family trip to the lake especially for Jenna. She loved being outside. Jenna loved pretty much everything. She didn't do a lot of talking. Mostly she smiled a lot and occasionally giggled. Jenna was born with Angelman syndrome, a rare genetic disorder that meant she would need intensive care for the rest of her life.

Acquaintances say that we also have two normal sons, 16-year-old Alex and 14-year-old Brian. They hate being called normal because it means that somehow Jenna was less than normal. They were very protective of their sister.

The day we lost Jenna, Alex and Brian were scouting around the island in the canoe. They're good boys. That day it was just my husband, Matt, Jenna and me in a rented rowboat. A canoe would have been too small for Jenna because the big circles she made with her arms when she got excited would have capsized such a little boat.

I should explain about my relationship with God and my understanding of faith. I had grown up the daughter of a pastor. My father's favorite Scripture was Hebrews 11:1. He made us kids learn it before we were old enough to go to kindergarten:

"Now faith is the substance of things hoped for, the

evidence of things not seen."

As a kid, I never understood the verse. To me, it was full of contradictions. I believed in God, or at least in a god. I didn't really know there was another option. But God had never shown himself to me. He had never delivered me from anything that my heart had hoped for. For instance, I had hoped, and even prayed that I would pass my 10th grade algebra test. I got a "D." I wasn't sure if I just didn't hope hard enough or wasn't specific enough. I had hoped a lot of things, but until I met Matt, life was mostly a series of small disappointments— just like I was a small disappointment to my parents.

I wasn't on drugs. I wasn't living a life of "sin". I wasn't angry with God, but I also didn't see how God really mattered in my day-to-day life. At some point, I stopped going to church. Not out of spite, but out of boredom. I stopped praying, too. I figured I could get a "D" without any divine intervention.

But, everything changed that day on the lake. I turned to Matt and asked him what kind of birds were squawking overhead. I thought they were geese. Matt looked up as the birds dashed across the lake in a classic flying-V formation and shouted something. I couldn't hear him over the birds.

I cupped my ear and yelled back, "What?!" "Canadian snow geese, I think!" he yelled back.

His yell seemed extra loud because the birds had moved on and the sound of their honking was fading. I turned back to Jenna to tell her about the Canadian snow geese.

She wasn't in the boat. I spotted her bright orange life jacket floating loose on the surface. I saw her fingers stretched out through the armhole before they slid under the glassy surface. I screamed and dove in after her.

I heard Matt plunk in the water as my head went under.

In the movies, the water is always so clear—like water a big bathtub. But in this water, I couldn't see anything. It was all a green fog. I swung my arms wildly. I felt flotsam slip through my fingers and past my body.

Time got away from me, so I couldn't gauge how long I was down there. But, my lungs were burning. All I could think was that if I was having such a hard time, how was Jenna going to survive? Was she scared? Was she flailing in a panic? Was she having one of her seizures?

I popped up above the water, right next to the orange life jacket. My head swiveled around. There was no sign of Matt anywhere. The boat was drifting farther away. I realized that it was much quieter above the water than under the water. Almost tranquil.

I dove back into the water, and, I guess, I prayed.

It wasn't like how I had learned to pray. I didn't even say the right words. There was no "God" or "Our Father Which Art in Heaven." It was just my heart pleading, begging, and hoping that I would find Jenna. Hoping that our angel was still with us.

What happened to me next is difficult to explain. Something, some force directed me to swim at a different angle and to swim deeper into the murky lake. It wasn't a voice. It wasn't even a feeling. It was as if some distant force was pushing me a different way.

I kept reaching around with my arms, hoping that as I swept them through the water, I would somehow make contact with Jenna. My lungs were burning again. I didn't have much time left. I was sure Jenna had even less time. I gave a big kick and dove down as deep as I could and swung my arms all around me.

Finally, I felt her arm. I grabbed it tight and pulled upwards. I reached around, still blind, and found her shirt with my other hand. I grabbed her, pulled her to me, and began kicking up at the same time.

I could see her blonde hair floating free. She didn't struggle. In that instant I wanted several things. I wanted to see her face. I wanted to breathe again, mostly I wanted to open my mouth and die under the water with my daughter.

I swam backward towards the boat, struggling to keep Jenna's face above the water. Every few minutes I screamed for Matt. I had this crazy thought that maybe he had succumbed to the water, like I had desperately wanted to moments before. I heard him pop up behind me. I yelled for him and he rushed over.

He took over towing Jenna while I clumsily tried to do CPR, while we were moving. When we reached the boat, it took both of us to get Jenna's lifeless body in. Matt rowed, and I started CPR in earnest.

This time I didn't pray or hope. I just did. I focused maniacally on every CPR technique I had ever learned. Right as we reached to dock, Jenna threw up a combination of water, bits of green plants, and the Lucky Charms from breakfast. She was alive.

Jenna was taken via helicopter to the hospital. I went with her while Matt stayed and gathered the boys.

Flying out of the mountains and down into the valley hospital, I realized that at 35, for the first time in my life, I understood what my father's favorite verse meant. I understood what the substance of things hoped for meant. I understood evidence of things unseen.

I still don't go to church much. I still don't understand God's role in my life. But, for the first time in my life, I have faith. I have touched the substance of hope. I now understand how you can have evidence of the intangible.

I lost my faith in my youth. I lost my Jenna. I found both under the murky water of the lake in the last place I would have ever looked on my own.

For Your Consideration

Use the space to answer the following question with as much truth and transparency as you can.

What do you put your faith in, and how strong is your faith?

MEDITATE ON THIS

Write the following quotation and Scripture in a journal. Then critically think about each one and write how each speaks to you. That is, how is each one renewing your mindset on the principle of faith being key to your fulfillment in life and spirituality?

Quotation

Faith: The thing that lies at the foundation of positive change, the way I see it, is service to a fellow human being.
- Lech Walesa

Scripture

Now faith is the substance of things hoped for, the evidence of things not seen.
Hebrews 11:1

Self-Assessment

*But let him ask in faith, with no doubting, for he who doubts
is like a wave of the sea driven and tossed by the wind.*
—James 1:6

Answer each question fully and to the best of your ability. Re member, because there are no judgments or wrong answers in whatever you write, strive to be transparent.

1. How does your faith help you with things unseen?

    _____
    _____
    _____
    _____

2. What role does faith play in your plans for the future?

    _____
    _____
    _____
    _____

3. Describe a faith-building moment in your life.

    _____
    _____
    _____
    _____

4. What is the relationship between faith and fulfillment in life?

    _____
    _____
    _____
    _____

TAKE ACTION

1. I will maintain my faith by

    _____
    _____
    _____
    _____

2. I will strengthen my faith by doing the following

    _____
    _____
    _____
    _____

3. I will express my faith by

    _____
    _____
    _____
    _____

    so that others will benefit from it.

GRATEFUL

A grateful heart is a beginning of greatness. It is an expression of humility. It is a foundation for the development of such virtues as prayer, faith, courage, contentment, happiness, love and well-being.

James E. Faust

GRATE·FUL

feeling or showing an appreciation of kindness;
being thankful

12

In the summer of 2018, the world anxiously held its breath as a very young Thai soccer team and their coach waited to be rescued from a cave that was nothing less than a system of crevices and caverns. This meant they could not easily navigate their way out of the cave as they did when they entered it to explore its surroundings and escape the heavy rain at the same time. In no time, the heavy rain flooded the dark cave. The team and their coach spent nine days waiting for a miracle while their food depleted as well as the oxygen level. Every breath they took became a miracle. What started out as a fun, post-practice adventure was turning into a fatal event. For sure, time was of the essence.

After considerable deliberation, cave rescue experts decided the best way to get them all out was to dive in and literally strap each one to a diver who would then swim out of the flooded cave system. The idea worked, and the boys and their coach were overwhelmed with gratitude, a feeling we have when we are grateful for something we could not make happen ourselves. In fact, being grateful implies positive life experiences for which we did not actively work towards or ask for. The boys and their coach did not hold back their eagerness to thank the divers—even the world—for the love and support extended their way. They realized that getting out of that cave was impossible for them had it not been for others coming to their rescue. Obviously, the inference here is that their outcome was out of their control and in the hands of others who did not disappoint. "I would like to thank everybody. You all love me and I love everyone," said Adul, one of the survivors. "I feel like people around the world are my parents[3]."

---

[3]https://www.goodmorningamerica.com/news/story/young-soccer-players-rescued-thai-cave-world-teaching-57331218

Grateful means appreciating something. You can be grateful for the way others treat you, or you can be grateful for the things you have. It means to recognize your blessings or good fortune. It is recognizing that you have benefited from someone else's kindness. Implied in all of this is that someone has had to *serve* you, and your proper response is being grateful for the service.

Surprisingly, most people cannot receive something gratefully. Society embraces the idea or thought that it is important to give, but more important to receive. In other words, selfishness has replaced the spirit of thanksgiving. And selfish people do not look for ways to serve others—as the rescue divers did. Many of those divers volunteered their talents to do something they knew those young boys and their coach could not do without their help. No wonder they were overwhelmed with gratitude when they were finally rescued. Their kind words about their rescuers show that when a person is grateful, they appreciate what is done for them and give thanksgiving accordingly. Contrarily when people are not grateful, they tend to ask for more all the time, like Veruca, the rich, ungrateful little girl in Roal Dahl's classic book, *Charlie and the Chocolate Factory*. While others in the story were experiencing desperate times, she and her family had more than enough. Yet Veruca wanted even more. As the story goes, her ingratitude leads to her demise as she demands more and more "Wonka bars" which held the famous golden tickets, until one day she is eventually sucked up by a pipe. One other ungrateful, unappreciative character in the same story meets with a tragic end. Greedy Augustus, who already had plenty of chocolate treats, falls into a chocolate river never to be seen again. In short, both characters met with an end that could have been avoided—had they been grateful for what they already had.

From the cave rescue story and Roald Dahl's fictional Willy

Wonka story, we see that being grateful has enormous, positive consequences. More specifically, being grateful likely brings more blessings your way, while being ungrateful terminates your chances of being shown further considerations from others.

Takeaways on Being Grateful

Appreciation is an aspect of being grateful. Being appreciative is never associated with an income level, social standing or education. It simply means one realizes the worth of another's efforts on his/her behalf and is consequently grateful for the service rendered. Appreciation is marked by a recognition that the source of goodness shown is outside of oneself. Again, nothing is required except "thank you".

Just like showing appreciation is a choice, the same is true for gratitude. Every day, we are all given a choice to express our gratitude: for seeing another day; for having family and friends who care about us; for being to work our gifts and talents for others; for the air we breathe, the water we drink; for acts of kindness shown to us; and for all the other graces shown to us over and over. When we are aware of our blessings, we tend to be grateful for them. We may even lean toward sharing our blessings with others, as the cave rescuers did with their ability to do the miraculous in dangerous situations. Which brings us to the next point.

Being grateful and showing the attitude of gratitude lead to fulfilled living because you are not focused on what's wrong about your life, but on what you can do to make things right for the lives of others. Fulfilled living has nothing to do with self-centeredness. Instead it's about sharing what you have (regardless of what it is) with others so that *their* outcomes change for the better. So then, being grateful has nothing to do with you. It has everything to do with others who extend themselves in ways that help you advance or to help you do something you could not on your own. All that is appreciated by you in return is genuine, continuous thanksgiving.

A Story about Being Grateful

Julia was one of the best civil rights lawyers in the country. She hated injustice. She fought hard for her clients. Despite the warnings of everyone around her, she took her cases very personally. It was what gave her the winning edge. She felt personally responsible for the future of her clients.

Julia was a fierce warrior. She viewed litigation as a war. She might not win every battle, but she intended to win every war.

Mostly, she did win. She had a bookcase of awards. She was well-respected by her colleagues; she was beloved by her clients and feared by those against whom she litigated.

But, Julia was not happy. She was angry. She was mostly angry with her grandfather.

Julia's grandfather, Raymond Leon Parks Jr., was the reason she had gone to law school in the first place. Before Julia was even born, Raymond had been convicted of a botched burglary that had resulted in three deaths. Raymond's daughter, Julia's mother, was just 12 years old at the time. The family knew Raymond hadn't committed the robbery because he was at home building a dollhouse while his daughter slept, and his wife worked the night shift at the diner.

Her path in life was set the first time she heard her grandfather's story. During college she convinced a law firm to look into her grandfather's case. The day before Julia graduated from law school, her grandfather was released from prison after serving nearly 38 years for a crime he did not commit.

Julia's excitement at her grandfather's release first turned into disappointment and then anger as she realized he was not mad about his incarceration. He was not filled with passionate desire to see justice done. He was not interested in seeking a monetary payout from the corrupt system that had unjustly imprisoned him. It seemed to Julia that all he ever did was express how grateful he was for everything.

He was grateful to be alive. He was grateful to be free. He was grateful for good food, a soft bed, and for the ability to listen to dusty old jazz records on sultry summer nights.

Julia was outraged by his lack of outrage. Getting her grandfather freed was not enough. She stoked the fires of her own anger until they burned hot enough for both her and her grandfather.

Raymond was living with his daughter, Julia's mother. Julia began to resent her mother for allowing Raymond to be so passive.

Why was he so happy? Why was he obsessed with saying how grateful he was for everything? The man had spent most of his adult life in prison for a crime he did not commit.

Julia routinely turned down her mother's invitations for get togethers. She was too busy with her work. She was too busy feeding her anger at the injustice of the world.

On Christmas Eve, business brought Julia to the town where her mother and grandfather were living. But, she didn't tell them she was there. She spent the day preparing for a series of important depositions that would start in three days.

Julia was reviewing police reports when her eyes stopped being able to focus. She tried to rub her eyes but found her hands wouldn't obey her commands. She tried to stand up, but she ended up collapsing on the floor.

The office she was working out of was barely staffed because of the holiday. Nobody knows exactly how long Julia lay on the floor before a legal assistant discovered her.

Julia woke up in a strange bed. It was a hospital bed. Julia was relieved that her eyes were able to focus. She tried to remember what had happened. Then she saw him—her grandfather. He was sitting in a chair, straight backed, humming softly to himself. When his eyes met hers, he smiled broadly and called out into the hall for Julia's mother.

Julia found out she had had a minor stroke. Her long-term prognosis was good, but she would have to learn to lower her stress. The idea of lowering her stress was the greatest source of distress for Julia for the next several weeks.

She was released from the hospital just days after waking up. She took medical leave from work and stayed in her childhood bedroom at her mother's house. She went to the doctor and the physical therapist every day. She seethed at the injustice of the stroke. She made little progress.

After one especially frustrating session where she was told that if she didn't learn to relax she would be dead in a year, her grandfather arrived to drive her home. He had just recently gotten his driver's license. He was grateful to be back behind the wheel.

Julia sat in the car in silence until Raymond turned the wrong way on the Lyman Parkway.

"Our house is the other way," Julia said. "I know," Raymond answered.

Confused, Julia asked, "Where are we going?"

"Julia, you rescued me from prison—and I am grateful for all your hard work. Now it's time for me to save you. Humor an old, broken down man and let me take you on a drive."

Julia nodded. She wanted to be angry, but instead she was just curious.

They ended up at the town cemetery. It was where her grandmother was buried. There was a light dusting of snow on the ground, but the sun was shining.

Raymond went around and opened the door for Julia and helped her out of the car. The two walked in silence to the bench that was directly opposite the grave of Julia's grandmother.

After a few minutes, Raymond turned to his granddaughter. "Julia," he began. "I know you think I should be angrier about what happened to me. But, I want you to understand something. I was angry. The first six months in prison I was a ball of rage. I plotted ways to escape. I tried to find ways to hurt the guards that kept me from my wife and my child. I was an angry man in a place filled with angry men."

Julia stared at her grandfather. She had never heard this story.

"One day my wife, your grandmother, came to visit. She could only afford to take the bus out to the prison once a month. Between traveling back and forth it took her all day just to visit with me for a couple of hours. She always brought our daughter, your mother, with her. But, this day she was alone."

Raymond cleared his throat and fought back tears. "'Where is my little girl', I asked her. She told me something that changed my life. She told me, 'Raymond you are the strongest man I know. But, you are broken. You have let them break you. I will not let your daughter see you a broken man. One day you will get out of here. I don't know when, but one day you will be free. Do you want to be a whole man or a broken man when you see your daughter? If you want to be whole, you have to let go of your anger. Find something to live for. Find something to be grateful for. That is the only way you will have the strength to be whole. Don't let them break you with hate.'"

Julia stared at the man about whom she now realized she knew so little.

"Julia, I chose that day to let go of my anger and my hatred. It was poisoning me. I promised myself that I would be grateful for what little I had. I soon found a lot of things to be grateful for. Being grateful kept me alive when the other prisoners rioted a few years later. It kept me from getting sentenced to even more time. Being grateful meant when you came along, I was able to go free. It also meant that I was able to be a whole man when I got out."

"Grandpa," Julia began, "I didn't know."

"I know, child. I don't like to talk about that place much. But, you are just as much a prisoner to your anger as I was to the State. It seems to me that you are mighty ungrateful for all the blessings and opportunities you have in this life. If you want to be locked up, then by all means, continue to rage. But, if you want to be free, you need to learn to be grateful."

No more words were spoken between the pair for several minutes. Finally, Julia, with tears in her eyes, grabbed her grandfather's arm.

"Thank you," Julia said.

Those two words changed Julia's life. She recovered her health. She continued her fight against injustice. But, it was with a new edge. She now was a happy warrior, grateful for all the small things in life.

For Your Consideration

Use the available space below to answer the question completely and transparently.

Why should you be grateful for an event that you did not cause?

MEDITATE ON THIS

Write the following quotation and Scripture in a journal. Then critically think about each one and write how each speaks to you. That is, how is each one renewing your mindset on the principle of being grateful as a key to your fulfillment in life and your spirituality?

Quotation

Be thankful for what you have; you'll end up having more. If you concentrate on what you don't have, you will never, ever have enough.
— Oprah Winfrey

Scripture

In everything give thanks; for this is the will of God in Christ Jesus for you.
1 Thessalonians 5:18

SELF-ASSESSMENT

Answer each question fully and to the best of your ability. Remember, because there are no judgments or wrong answers in whatever you write, strive to be transparent.

1. Describe a relationship for which you are grateful. Be sure to include why you are grateful for this relationship.

   _____
   _____
   _____
   _____

2. How do you measure gratefulness? If you do not believe it can be measured, explain why.

   _____
   _____
   _____
   _____

3. When was the last time you expressed gratefulness? How do others know you are grateful?

   _____
   _____
   _____
   _____

TAKE ACTION

1. I will consistently show that I am grateful by doing the following

   _____

   _____

   _____

   _____

2. What actions will you take in your present spiritual development to grow your degree of gratefulness?

   _____

   _____

   _____

   _____

3. How will you shift your focus from yourself to others?

   _____

   _____

   _____

   _____

THE AFTERWORD

Sticks and stones may break my bones, but words will never hurt me.

As a kid, I remember chanting this as my go-to comeback whenever someone's negative words got to the core of my soul and just kind of hung there. It was the only response I could think of to self-medicate from the sting of that person's words. I am an adult now, but like many of you, I have learned that this age-old streetwise response to a bully's taunts is not true at all. Words *can* hurt. They even pack the power to keep you broken for years and years. In fact, nearly every word we pass forward is on a mission to either heal well or cut deeply, depending upon the motive (or mood) of the user. For me as a pastor, the big picture is this: it matters a great deal what we pass on to people, including our words. Take younger generations, for example. If we as parents, teachers, community and faith-based leaders, mentors, policy makers, etc., neglect to pass on to them words that encourage, build relationships, express love and concern, motivate, inspire and so on, then we are failing to equip generations of people with the capacity to support one another. Can you imagine what it would be like to live in a society where people do not know how to get along because they were not taught to instill life into others with just the power of their words? With our words alone, we can change the trajectory of things for our young. Think about it. Consider how often we parents, for instance, speak to our children. What we say to them, how we say it, and how much time we take to listen to them matter to their outcomes when they are adults who, in turn, will be able to do the same thing. And, it all begins with words.

With the ever-increasing rise in bullying on elementary and

high school campuses, I am also concerned about young people not having the mindset to pass on all things positive. I am aware that they spend an inordinate amount of time on various social media, which seem to be the preferred platforms to pass on meanness. This is unsettling for two reasons. One is that some of us tend to think that passing on mean words is something people outgrow. Let me assure you, it is not, which brings me to reason two. In 2018, growing research[4] suggests that these young bullies matriculate out of primary education right into post-secondary education settings where they continue to pass on hurtful words. Since we know that meanness does not end in high school, I would like to think that that is incentive enough for us to teach our young the power of words. And those lessons need to start from the cradle. The sooner the better.

Finally, I want to return to something we mentioned in an earlier chapter. In it, we encouraged you to level up on your language. You can start by transforming the way you tend to look at your outcomes. For instance, instead of thinking things will never work out for you, *begin speaking* that they will change for your good. Since your tongue will not betray what your mind thinks, then transforming the mindset precedes transforming your language.

If we truly concern ourselves with the power that word choices have over children, I believe we would be more concerned about how they process what we say to them as well as other behaviors we exhibit around them. As a pastor who has advised many people who were hurt over words said to them, I know the lasting effect that words can have over people's lives.

---

[4] Retrieved from the internet https://www.verywell-family.com/facts-about-college-bullying-460487, November 8, 2018, 7:35PM.

People tend to internalize what they hear, so if the words they hear are positive and life-giving, then those words will motivate them to pass on good…all the time.

RESOURCES

Chapman, Gary. Love as a Way of Life: Seven Keys to Transforming Every Aspect of Your Life. Doubleday Religion Hardcover, 2008.

Brainyquote.com; Colin Powell Quotes; https://www.brainyquote.com/search_results?q=There%20are%20no%20secrets%20to%20success.%20It%20is%20the%20result%20of%20preparation%E2%80%A6.

Goodreads.com; John F. Kennedy; Quotes; Quotable Quote; https://www.goodreads.com/quotes/131933-the-time-to-repair-the-roof-is-when-the-sun

Jain, Naveen, "The Great Face of Humility in an Unlikely Place, December 20, 2012, https://www.forbes.com/sites/naveenjain/2012/12/20/richard-branson-naveen-jain-the-great-face-of-humility/#704fb40473cb.

"Full Circle", CNN Interview with Anderson Cooper and Geoffrey Owens, September 5, 2018, https://www.cnn.com/videos/tv/2018/09/05/geoffrey-owens-acfc-cnntv.cnn

Goodreads.com; Roy T. Bennett Quotes; https://www.goodreads.com/quotes/7883124-it-takes-guts-and-humility-to-admit-mistakes-admitting-we-re

Goodreads.com; Winston Churchill Quotes; https://www.goodreads.com/work/quotes/46847927

Goodreads.com; A.A. Milne Quotes; https://www.goodreads.com/quotes/search?utf8=%E2%9C%93&q=A.A.+Milne&commit=Search

Proverbia.com; Authors; Douglas Adams;

http://en.proverbia.net/citasautor.asp?autor=10030

Bloom, Steve, "7 Reasons Why Helping Others Will Make You Live a Better Life," September 21, 2018, 10:43 PM. http://dosomethingcool.net/helping-others-life/www.dosomethingcool.net/helping-others-life/

Goodreads.com; Ramana Maharshi Quotes; https://www.goodreads.com/quotes/search?utf8=%E2%9C%93&q=Ramana+Maharshi&commit=Search

Goodreads.com; Helen Keller Quotes; https://www.goodreads.com/quotes/search?utf8=%E2%9C%93&q=helen+keller&commit=Search

Goodreads.com; Ahmir Questlove Thompson; Quotes; Quotable Quote; https://www.goodreads.com/quotes/9285109-collaborations-work-best-this-way-when-there-s-a-mutual-desire

Caron Butler, text message to author, October 7, 2017.

Auclair, T.J., "Tiger Woods' comebacks: A history of fighting his way back to the top," PGA.com, Monday, November 26, 2018, 1:24 PM. https://www.pga.com/news/pga-tour/tiger-woods-comeback-history

Goodreads.com; Never Give Up Quotes; https://www.goodreads.com/quotes/tag/never-give-up

Robison, Jennifer, "Saving Campbell Soup Company: How a high-energy leader turned around this iconic business by winning in the workplace -- and the marketplace - A Q&A with Douglas R. Conant, President and Chief Executive Officer of Campbell Soup Company, News.Gallup.com, February 11, 2010. https://news.gallup.com/businessjournal/125687/saving-campbell-soup-company.aspx

Whipple, Bob, "Articles: Trust but Verify," Leadergrow.com,

undated. https://www.leadergrow.com/articles/443-trust-but-verify

Quote Investigator, "They May Forget What You Said, But They Will Never Forget How You Made Them Feel", undated. https://quoteinvestigator.com/2014/04/06/they-feel/

National Space Agency (NSA), NSA.gov, January 28, 2013. https://www.nasa.gov/multimedia/imagegallery/image_gall ery_2437.html

Luis-Watson, Judy, "The Challenger's Teacher in Space Project: Photos and Video," January 27, 2016. https://unwritten-record.blogs.archives.gov/2016/01/27/the-challengers-teacher-in-space-project-photos-and-video/

Craig Robinson, email message to author, December 12, 2018.

Halper, Daniel, "Michelle Obama to Chicago Grads: 'You Have More Scars Than They Do'", Weekly Standard.com, June 10, 2015. https://www.weeklystandard.com/daniel-halper/michelle-obama-to-chicago-grads-you-have-more-scars-than-they-do

Goodreads.com; Dr. Martin Luther King, Jr, Quotes, Quotable Quote; https://www.goodreads.com/quotes/202045-true-peace-is-not-merely-the-absence-of-tension-it

Goodreads.com; Dr. Wayne W. Dyer; Quotes; Quotable Quote; https://www.goodreads.com/quotes/548799-peace-is-the-result-of-retraining-your-mind-to-process

Goodreads.com; Kahlil Gibran; Quotes; Quotable Quotes; https://www.goodreads.com/quotes/273408-faith-is-a-knowledge-within-the-heart-beyond-the-reach

Brainyquote.com; Lech Walesa Quotes; https://www.brainyquote.com/quotes/lech_walesa_160617

Faust, Elder James E., The Church of Jesus Christ of the Latter Day Saints; LDS.org; November 1993.

https://www.lds.org/new-era/1993/11/an-attitude-of-gratitude?lang=eng

Hutchinson, Bill, and Longman, James, "Boys rescued from Thai cave 'overwhelmed' when divers first arrived", August 22, 2018. https://www.goodmorningamerica.com/news/story/young-soccer-players-rescued-thai-cave-world-teaching-57331218

Brainyquote.com; Oprah Winfrey Quotes; https://www.brainyquote.com/quotes/oprah_winfrey_163087

Gordon, Sherri, "5 Facts About Bullying in College," Verywellfamily.com, updated March 27, 2018. https://www.verywell-family.com/facts-about-college-bullying-460487

Dahl, Roald. Charlie and the Chocolate Factory. Alfred A. Knopf, Inc. United Kingdom. 1964.

The Holy Bible, King James Version. Public Domain.

The Holy Bible: The New King James Version. Thomas Nelson. Nashville. 1982.

The Holy Bible, New International Version. Zondervan House. Grand Rapids. 1984.

ACKNOWLEDGEMENTS

There is no such thing as reaching success on your own. Somewhere along the way, someone has helped you. Humbled by that truth, we wish to thank the following people for their graciousness and assistance in bringing our vision to replace negative words with positive, healthful ones.

From DeNita,

To my mentor, Pastor John Jenkins, thank you for helping me see the added value in service. Your infinite wisdom has enriched my life.

From Pastor Jenkins,

To my loving wife, Trina, of 38 years, I am eternally grateful for your love and support. Your tireless love and devotion make it possible for me to venture into areas that otherwise would be impossible.

To my family, thank you for your patience, love and support. I am so grateful and proud to call you mine.

To my church family and friends at First Baptist Church of Glenarden, thank you for the motivation and inspiration that you provide me on a regular basis. I appreciate all of you!

To my co-author, DeNita, thank you for all of the work that you have done to bring this goal to fruition. Your passion and support are unparalleled. Thank you for your relentless dedication to this project. You are a jewel.

From DeNita and John

To our team that worked tirelessly to bring us over the finish line—Fountaine, Derek, Inez, Kate, Jon, Aunt Joe, and Walt. Thank you for your loyal support, contributions, and loving spirit!

CPSIA information can be obtained
at www.ICGtesting.com
Printed in the USA
LVHW012127210519
618618LV00017B/1247/P

9 780578 213873